STRETCHY
LIBRARY LESSONS

Multicultural Activities

Pat Miller

UpstartBooks

Fort Atkinson, Wisconsin

For Aileen Kirkham,
who speaks friendship in several languages.

With thanks to Michelle McCardell, my patient and positive editor,
and Heidi Green, Upstart's magical art director.

Credits:
Pages 69–72: Cat and Rat adapted from the book *Cat and Rat: The Legend of the Chinese Zodiac* by Ed Young, published by Henry Holt & Co. Copyright © 1995 by Ed Young.

Published by UpstartBooks
W5527 Highway 106
P.O. Box 800
Fort Atkinson, Wisconsin 53538-0800
1-800-448-4887

Contents

Introduction

Immigrants have been coming to this country for thousands of years. When they discovered a land bridge to present-day Alaska, men and women from Asia walked into the land we now call the United States. The stream of immigrants from all over the world continues to this day.

Worldwide diversity is also represented in the quality literature that is published every year in this country. Authors and illustrators from many cultures are making an impact with their work. Fiction represents the experiences of every culture and touches the hearts of the readers, putting them into the shoes of one who experiences life from a different perspective. Nonfiction provides supplemental information for curious students who hear the news, meet friends from other cultures or encounter new countries in their studies or their reading.

The literature chosen for this book addresses the universal themes and values that underlie every culture. Students will identify with a child's love of his or her home, whether that home is in Somalia or Scranton. Every child knows what it is like to be left out of a group because of language, clothes or just because he or she is "the new kid." We all get hungry, we all dress for the weather and we all like to play. How we meet these needs varies around the world, and provides for fascinating information to share with students. These books include cultural details that help the reader experience the emotion, event or character from a perspective that may be different from the reader's.

Book selections include resources about children from various cultures, living in this country and in their homeland. I included nonfiction for background and poetry for flavor. Lessons include a related bibliography, with annotations and suggested grade levels. Use these books to extend the lesson, or to modify it up or down for students who are older or younger than the lesson books.

Cultures represented are those most prevalent in our schools today. Sharing cultures not only extends understanding, it makes the children of that culture feel affirmed and accepted. I discovered in my own lesson planning that I was inadvertently leaning on anthropomorphic animal stories. Hopefully, this collection with its new ideas will help you balance and enrich your current program.

This book is not designed to teach about cultures, but to teach about universality and the richness added by the differences various cultural groups bring to your own world. No matter what groups are represented at your school, the experiences and perspectives shared in this book will be ones they can identify with and hopefully absorb as respect for various approaches to the process of living that we all share.

The Stretchy Library Lessons series, of which this is the fourth book, is designed to give you ideas for adapting lessons to fit your time constraints. The lessons cross the elementary grade levels, provide numerous ways to pack a lot of learning into each lesson and extend short lessons with a variety of literature and activities.

How to Use This Book

Stretchy Library Lessons: Multicultural Activities has 10 basic lessons that can be stretched into 20 or more lessons, depending on the number of resources you choose to use. All of the lessons are purposely designed to appeal to multiple intelligences, learning styles and reading abilities. The skills index on page 8 correlates each lesson by grade level and skill.

Rather than saving cultural selections for a particular month or holiday, use them consistently. These books were chosen for their universal themes, so they fit with your curriculum and make a variety of cultures seem like an important ingredient in, rather than just sprinkles on, the frosting of life.

Each Stretchy Library Lesson includes:

- **Grades.** The lessons are K–5, though they can be adapted for preschoolers, special needs students and sixth graders.

- **A Purpose.** This helps library media specialists integrate the lessons with class curriculum, district and state media literacy standards and social and emotional goals.

- **The Format.** Listing the format (game, contest, read-aloud, etc.) helps you appeal to different learning styles and intelligences.

- **A List of Materials.** These are readily available or easily made and should be gathered before you teach the lesson.

- **Items to Prepare in Advance.** If you teach all grades each day as I do, your lesson materials need to be well organized because there is little time between classes. This section tells you what needs to be made, purchased or found before a class comes in.

- **Activity Directions.** The basic lessons can be taught in 20–30 minutes. The activities include all forms, worksheets and patterns that you will need.

- **The Stretchy Activity.** This activity extends the lesson to fit a longer time frame. If you have short classes like I do, the lessons in this book may be enough for 20 sessions. The stretchy activities include their own materials list, items to prepare in advance and steps for teaching the lesson.

- **Resources.** These books can be used instead of the featured title or as an extension. I tried to include newer works, all of which are in print and available from bookstores or on-line at press time. Always put these or similar books on display near your teaching area in case a teacher or child wants to extend their learning.

Give this magic carpet bookmark to your students as you challenge them to read around the world!

Key Reading Skills

1. Listen and speak to gain knowledge of his or her own culture, the culture of others and the common elements of cultures.

2. Connect his or her own experiences, information, insights and ideas with those of others through speaking and listening.

3. Use a variety of rich materials including biography, folktales, poetry, songs, fiction and nonfiction.

4. Identify customs, celebrations and traditions of various culture groups in the United States.

5. Identify similarities and differences within and among selected racial, ethnic and religious groups in the United States.

6. Summarize the contribution of people of various racial, ethnic and religious groups to our national identity.

7. Identify family customs, traditions, beliefs and languages, and explain their similarities and differences across cultures.

8. Compare language and oral traditions that reflect customs, regions and cultures.

9. Identify and describe similarities and differences between the ways cultures meet their needs for food, clothing, shelter and employment.

10. Practice acceptance of and respect for a variety of ways of doing, believing, speaking and behaving.

Grade Appropriate Skills Index

The main activities are in bold.

LESSON TITLE	GRADES							SKILLS									
	K	1	2	3	4	5		1	2	3	4	5	6	7	8	9	10
Many Cultures	X	X	X	X	X	X		X	X			X		X		X	X
All the Same, All Different	X	X	X	X	X	X			X			X					X
Fitting In	X	X	X	X				X	X			X					X
It Happened Again	X	X	X	X				X	X			X				X	X
Men of Peace				X	X	X				X		X	X				X
From India			X	X	X	X		X		X			X				X
Turning the Tables				X	X	X		X		X	X		X	X			
Student Storytelling				X	X	X		X		X					X		X
Counting Seasons			X	X	X	X					X		X		X		X
Seasonal Clothing				X	X	X		X								X	
Honesty	X	X	X	X	X			X	X								
Perseverance	X	X	X	X				X	X						X		
Kids Just Want to Have Fun	X	X	X					X	X		X	X					X
Galimoto	X	X	X	X				X				X					
Mama Provi and the Pot of Rice	X	X	X						X							X	X
World of Food				X	X	X							X			X	
The Squeaky Door	X	X	X					X	X						X		
Cruise to Puerto Rico				X	X	X			X			X	X				
Chinese New Year			X	X	X	X		X				X	X				
Cat and Rat Reader's Theater			X	X	X	X		X		X					X		X

A Global Community

Many Cultures

MAIN ACTIVITY

Grades: K–5

Purposes:

- To make students aware, in a non-didactic way, that people all over the world have similarities in their emotions, thoughts and behaviors.

- To develop feelings of empathy and respect for those new to our country.

- To think about the legacy each child has in his or her character from ancestors.

- To realize that the contributions of many cultures make our lives richer than a homogeneous culture would be.

Format: Writing Exercise, Craft Activity

Materials:

- *Momma, Where Are You From?* by Marie Bradby (Scholastic, 2000)

- chart on blackboard or overhcad transparency

- copies of Where Are You From? worksheet on page 13 for student use

- map to locate Somalia and/or China
  (www.nationalgeographic.com/xpeditions/atlas/index.html)

Prepare in Advance: Reproduce the chart on a transparency. Discuss the activity with the teacher prior to class. If he or she is agreeable to the idea, make enough copies for each student so they can continue the writing exercise in class.

Activity Directions:

1. Ask students "Where are you from?" They may answer with their address, country of origin, state or family name. Tell them all are correct, but even more important is **who** they come from and the experiences and wisdom of all who came before them in their families.

2. Read *Momma, Where Are You From?* and share the vibrant illustrations. In this story, a daughter asks the question as she snaps beans with her mother in their sunny kitchen. The illustrations that follow show Momma's forebears doing activities that have made her the person she is. "I'm from Monday mornings, washing loads of clothes in the wringer washer …" Some of the memories are sad, some are funny and all involve family.

At the end of the book, the daughter realizes that she is "that morning-washing, bean-snapping … star-dreaming girl. That's where I'm from."

3. As a group, brainstorm some of the descriptions students could use to describe themselves in the same ways. To get them thinking, show the chart categories on a chalkboard or overhead projector. Each response should include a verb or an adjective as well as the nouns.

All the Same, All Different

Materials:

- simple die-cut figure for each student (star, bell, boot)

- markers

- rubber stamps and pads

- crayons

- stickers

- creative hole punches (ask your scrapbooking teachers)

- other decorative items

- collection boxes

Prepare in Advance: Cut die-cuts for every student and teacher. Collect art supplies. Set up student workstations that include supplies for decorating their figure and a collection box.

Activity Directions:

1. Discuss the ways all of us are alike. Discuss ways we are different. Be specific. You might ask how many like pickles and peanut butter, how many would not want a snake for a pet, how many are only children, etc., to get the discussion started. Our similarities make us comfortable; our differences make our lives richer.

2. Have students write their name on the front of their figure. Then give them a short amount of time to arrange the die-cuts. When the time is up, hang the stars in a bulletin board firmament, leaves on bare tree branches, bells on ribbons strung across the bulletin board, etc. Have students note how all the figures are different, even though everyone had the same directions, the same figure and the same supplies. What makes the difference? It's our individuality and creativity.

3. You may also play a fun game that will emphasize similarities and differences. Arrange enough chairs for all the players but one in a circle facing in. One player stands in the center and says, "Who is like me because they like cats?" or "Who is different from me because they like dogs?" Students who can answer the question "I am" stand and change

seats with someone else who answers the question. The student in the center also tries to claim a seat. Players may not take a seat on either side of them. Remind the students of the rules of behavior. You might want to begin with yourself, then remove your chair and select the next caller. If students have difficulty thinking of categories, suggest one for them. Here are some suggestions:

Who is the same as me because they like to chew bubble gum?

Who is the same as me because they like to read for fun?

Who is the same as me because they hate to shop for clothes?

Who is the same as me because they have two brothers?

Who is different from me because they like chocolate milk?

Who is different from me because they have seen the Statue of Liberty?

Who is different from me because they like dogs better than cats?

Who is different from me because they have gone to summer camp?

Resources

Professional Books:

Connecting Cultures: A Guide to Multicultural Literature for Children by Rebecca L. Thomas. R. R. Bowker, 1996. The literature in this book is indexed six ways: annotated bibliography, subject access, title index, illustrator index, culture index and use-level index (appropriate grade levels).

Cultural Awareness for Children by Judy Allen, Earldene McNeill, Velma Schmidt. Addison-Wesley, 1992. The Learning Tree School is a school in Dallas that has been teaching multicultural perspectives since 1970. This book is the outgrowth of all they have learned and taught. Chapters include African and African American, American Indian, Japanese and Japanese American, Korean and Korean American, Chinese and Chinese American, Mexican and Mexican American, Thai and Southeast Asian Cultures. Each unit includes information and creative activities based on homes, clothing, food, decorative arts, animals, plants, folktales, language, music and dance, games and manipulatives and special events and celebrations. Extensive lists of books, magazines, media, materials and professional books end each unit.

The World Through Children's Books edited by Susan Stan. Rowman & Littlefield Publishers, 2002. This annotated bibliography is organized by geographical region and country. It includes international children's books published between 1996 and 2000, as well as selected books published in the United States but set in another country.

Books:

The Great Round-the-World Balloon Race by Sue Scullard. Dutton Children's Books, 1991. (K–3) Harriet Shaw and her niece and nephew enter a balloon race that begins in Paris. The homeland of each entrant is mentioned as well as the countries they visit. The end page is a spread of the race route.

Give students a world map that names countries. As you read, help students track the balloon race using an overhead projector.

Momma, Where Are You From? by Marie Bradby. Scholastic, 2000. (K–2) Momma describes the special people and surroundings of her childhood, in a place where the edge of town met the countryside, in a time when all the children at school were brown.

Web sites:

How to Choose the Best Multicultural Books
teacher.scholastic.com/lessonrepro/lessonplans/instructor/multicultural.htm
Five articles which include reviews of 10 children's books for K–8, advice from a multicultural author or illustrator (Joseph Bruchac, Gary Soto, Floyd Cooper, Patricia Polacco and Yumi Heo), key criteria to use when selecting books and notable authors in that culture. Cultures include: Native Americans, Latinos, African Americans, Jews and Asian Americans.

Multicultural Calendar
www.kidlink.org/KIDPROJ/MCC
Entries can be searched by month, holiday or country. Children submit entries about how they celebrate their holidays. They may share background information, significance of the holidays and the special ways in which these days are observed.

Peace Corps Kids World: Explore the World
www.peacecorps.gov/kids/world
Click on a continent, then a country to learn all about it in kid-friendly language.

Where Are You From?

Family Chores	Family Favorite Foods	Family Favorite Things to Buy	Family Fun

School

Fitting In

MAIN ACTIVITY

Grades: K–3 (For grades 4–5, read aloud one of the chapter books listed in the resource list and discuss it, or use a picture book to kick off a discussion of when students were new themselves and what that was like.)

Purposes:

• To become aware that knowledge brings understanding, and lack of it causes us to fear or reject that which we don't understand.

• To understand that we are each like a puzzle piece, trying to fit in, and important to "the big picture."

Format: Read Aloud and Discussion

Materials:

• a 100 piece puzzle with an interesting picture on the box (The pieces will be given away. Be sure you have enough pieces for all classes.)

• *The Color of Home* by Mary Hoffman (Penguin Putnam, 2002)

• *Yoko* by Rosemary Wells (Hyperion, 1998)

• world map to locate Somalia, Japan and your hometown

Prepare in Advance: Gather books and other "new to school" titles and set up a display in a reading corner. Bring in puzzles. (This is a good opportunity to get rid of your puzzles that are missing pieces.)

Activity Directions:

1. Talk to students about a time they were the new student in their class. Do they remember the person who first became their friend? Do they remember an incident that embarrassed them or caused them to feel confused?

2. Read aloud one of the two books in the materials list.

3. What do you think Yoko's / Hassan's classmates thought of her or him when they first saw her lunch / saw how quiet and confused he seemed? How did Timothy / Jake make a difference to his classmate? How can we do the same for the new students in our classes?

4. Give students a puzzle piece and show them the picture on the box. Make the analogy that each of us is like a piece of the puzzle. We are all different, but we hope to fit in, and without each of us, the big picture is incomplete.

It Happened Again

S·T·R·E·T·C·H·Y ACTIVITY

Materials:

- the book you did not use in the previous lesson

- compare/contrast chart

Prepare in Advance: Draw a Venn diagram on the board or overhead projector. Label each circle with the title of the books you shared with students.

Activity Directions:

1. Read the second book.

2. Have students suggest similarities and differences between Hassan's and Yoko's story.

3. Encourage students to relate similar incidents that happened to them, either because they were new or because they helped another to "fit in."

Resources

Books:

Angel Child, Dragon Child by Michele Maria Surat. Scholastic, 1990. (K–3) Ut tries to be an angel child, as her mother urged her when Ut came to America. But when the children tease her, or a bully hits her sister with a snowball, Ut becomes a dragon child. Eventually, her classmates help arrange a Vietnam Fair to raise money to bring Ut's mother to the United States. Correct pronunciation of Vietnamese words is at the bottom of each page.

Back to School by Maya Ajmera and John D. Ivanho. Charlesbridge Publishing, 2001. (K–2) Photographs and text describe the experiences of school children from 37 countries. From arriving at school, perhaps in a horse-drawn wagon in Bolivia, to what students wear, eat and do at school, readers will get a world peek at school kids from Iraq, Mali, South Africa and 34 other countries.

The Color of Home by Mary Hoffman. Penguin Putnam, 2002. (K–3) Hassan is a refuge from Somalia who doesn't feel at home at this school that is held indoors. He doesn't eat the lunch because he doesn't know the foods and he doesn't understand the language. It is not until his teacher gives him paints that he can express himself. Through a translator, Hassan tells about his life in the Somali home he loved and how the soldiers came. After playing soccer with new friend Jake, Hassan paints a happy picture of his new home.

Dear Whiskers by Ann Whitehead Nagda. Holiday House, 2000. (2–5) Jenny is discouraged when her second grade pen pal won't write back. She discovers that the child is a silent new girl from Saudi Arabia. Jenny wishes she had gotten a more likable child, but she discovers the secret to overcoming Sameera's shyness and fear.

I Hate English by Ellen Levine. Scholastic, 1995. (K–3) Mei Mei misses Hong Kong and has trouble adjusting to New York City, her school and the foreign sounds of the impossible language called English.

In English, Of Course by Josephine Nobisso. Gingerbread House, 2002. (2–4) Josephine, an Italian immigrant to the Bronx, inadvertently makes her class think she was raised on a farm when she tries to tell them of her farm visit in English. Her teacher and classmates help her overcome her frustration.

Kirsten Learns A Lesson: A School Story by Janet Beeler Shaw. Pleasant Company Publications, 1986. (3–5) Learning in a prairie school is different from her Swedish home, and Kirsten is helped by her secret friendship with a Native American girl.

Look What Came From Japan by Miles Harvey. Scholastic Library Publishing, 1999. (2–5) Describes many things which originated in Japan, including inventions, art, food, fashion, furniture, toys, animals, musical instruments and sports.

Put this list of items on an overhead transparency, and ask students to guess which have come to us from Japan. (Answers: all except paper, invented in China, and fortune cookies and Chinese jump rope, invented in the U.S.)

pottery	novels	futon
fortune cookies	mushrooms	paper
kimono	CD-ROM	judo
DVD	Chinese jump rope	sukiyaki
VCR	haiku	Origami
soy sauce	sushi	sumo wrestling

Molly's Pilgrim by Barbara Cohen. William Morrow & Co., 1998. (3–5) Molly is embarrassed when her mother tries to help by making a pilgrim doll for the Thanksgiving display at school. Her mother dresses the doll as she herself was dressed before leaving Russia to seek religious freedom.

My Name is Maria Isabel by Alma Flor Ada. Simon & Schuster, 1995. (2–4) Maria Isabel Salazar Lopez is called Mary at school because there are two other Marias in her class. Because she forgets to answer to "Mary," Maria gets in trouble and is even excluded from the school's winter pageant. Maria summons her pride in her heritage and her wits to figure out the solution to her miseries at school.

My Name is Yoon by Helen Recorvits. Farrar, Straus and Giroux, 2003. (K–3) A young Korean feels dislocated and homesick. The story will help readers/listeners feel empathy for new students and their struggle to fit in, whether they are from another school or another country.

Yoko by Rosemary Wells. Hyperion, 1998. (K–3) Yoko is enjoying her first day at school until it's time for lunch. Her friends have peanut butter and honey, Swiss cheese on rye and beans and franks. When Yoko unpacks her lunch of sushi and red bean ice cream, they say, "Ick!" and "Yuck-o-rama!" and Yoko is hurt. Her teacher comes up with an idea that doesn't make things perfect, but paves the way for a new friendship.

Web sites:

Connect with Kids and Parents of Different Cultures
teacher.scholastic.com/professional/teachdive/connectcultures.htm
This article contains excellent suggestions for making parents from other cultures feel involved and welcome in their children's classroom.

Crayola Card Creator
www.crayola.com/cardcreator/index.cfm?mt=cardcreator
Select and personalize a card to print off for a new friend.

Crayola Creativity Central: Make New Friends
www.crayola.com/educators/lessons/display.cfm?id=498
Directions for a crayon project that focuses on friendship skills as students think about how to introduce themselves to others and what makes a good friend.

Peace Corps Kids' World: Foods, Friends and Fun
www.peacecorps.gov/kids/like/
What would it be like to go to school in Nepal? How would it be if your father got transferred to Kirabati and you had to go to school there?

Important Contributions

Men of Peace

Grades: 3–5

Purposes:

- To compare the lives of Dr. Martin Luther King Jr. and Mahatma Gandhi.

- To learn how nonviolence has affected great change in our country and in the world.

Format: Read Aloud, Group Participation

Materials:

- *Martin's Big Words: The Life of Dr. Martin Luther King Jr.* by Doreen Rappaport (Hyperion, 2001)

- *Gandhi* by Demi (M. K. McElderry Books, 2001)

- other books on Dr. King and Mahatma Gandhi

- world map to locate India, South Africa and United States/Georgia.

Prepare in Advance: Prepare the transparency on page 21. Duplicate the question sheet for use with students. Read both books.

Activity Directions:

1. Show the children the chart. Ask them to listen for the answers to each category as you read.

2. Read *Martin's Big Words* to your students and allow time for discussion after. As students hear answers, they can raise their hands to stop the story. Jot down the answers as students supply them.

3. Repeat with *Gandhi.*

4. When the chart is complete, ask students to tell you what they notice about the lives of the two men.

From India

S·T·R·E·T·C·H·Y ACTIVITY

Materials:

- *Look What Came From India* by Miles Harvey (Scholastic Library Publishing, 1999)

- India questions (see below)

- world map to locate India

Prepare in Advance: Photocopy the questions below and put them near your teaching area. Set up a display of books about India.

Activity Directions:

1. Before reading the book to students, ask the following questions. Students should indicate **True** with thumbs up, **False** with thumbs down and thumbs sideways if they don't know.

   India has more people than any other country.
   False. It is the second largest. One person out of every six in the world is from India.

   India is one of the oldest countries on Earth.
   True. Their civilization dates back over 5,000 years.

   The first bathroom was invented in ancient India.
   True. They also invented toilets made of bricks with wooden seats.

   Which of the following first came from India? *(thumbs up = yes, thumbs down = no)*

pepper	sugar	salt *(no)*
mangoes	plastic surgery	chess *(no)*
Parcheesi	pajamas	

   Which of these animals live in India?
   (thumbs up = yes, thumbs down = no) (all of them do)

Indian cobra	Indian elephant	Indian rhinoceros
Bengal tiger	Pygmy hog	Sloth bear

2. Do not answer the questions. Instead, read the book or the appropriate passages from the book so students can see if they are correct. (Questions are listed in the order in which the answers will be heard or read in the book.)

Resources

Books:

People from many cultures and countries have made important contributions to the quality of life for their countrymen and for the world. You may want to share the following books with your students:

The Boy Who Drew Cats: A Japanese Folktale by Margaret Hodges. Holiday House, 2002. (2–4) This is the fictionalized story about the childhood of the artist Soshu Toyo, who loved to draw cats and who, the story has it, was saved by the cats he drew.

Confucius: The Golden Rule by Russell Freedman. Scholastic, 2002. (3–5) Although Confucius (Kongfuzi in China), who lived 2,500 years ago, did not found a religion, many of his beliefs echo in religious traditions that came after him. The Golden Rule of Christianity sounds much like Confucius's teaching: "Do not impose on others what you do not wish for yourself." His political beliefs were based on merit rather than inheritance and they are echoed in the preamble to the American Constitution. This biography would be an excellent one to read aloud during the study of the U.S. system of government.

Cool Melons—Turn to Frogs! The Life and Poems of Issa by Matthew Gollub. Lee & Low Books, 1998. (3–5) The life of Issa is told with poems interspersed that reflect something from that time in his life. The author's note adds more information about the poet and the collaboration between American author/translator and the Japanese illustrator.

Diego: In English and Spanish by Jeanette Winter. Bantam Doubleday Dell, 1994. (K–3) This biography is told in one or two sentences per page, in both languages, with colorful illustrations. Diego Rivera became famous for painting murals on public walls all over Mexico. In his life, he painted more than two and a half miles of murals.

Gandhi by Hitz Demi. M. K. McElderry Books, 2001. (3–5) Demi captures the spirit that was Mahatma Gandhi and pays homage to this great man.

Look What Came from India by Miles Harvey. Scholastic Library Publishing, 1999. (3–5) Describes many familiar things that originally came from India.

Martin's Big Words: The Life of Dr. Martin Luther King Jr. by Doreen Rappaport. Hyperion, 2001. (3–5) Dr. Martin Luther King Jr.'s message of love, justice and freedom shines through every page of this book.

Web sites:

Biography of Mahatma Gandhi
search.biography.com/print_record.pl?id=5148
Read more details about the Father of India who inspired millions.

Dr. Martin Luther King Interactive Scavenger Hunt
users.rcn.com/tstrong.massed/Martin.htm
Questions include Web sites to locate the answers. A teacher's guide is included.

Research Tools: Martin Luther King Jr. and African American History
teacher.scholastic.com/researchtools/articlearchives/honormlk/index.htm
This page of sites includes the life and words of MLK, a play, quotes from Dr. King, Civil Rights articles and timeline and biographies of notable African Americans.

Men of Peace

	Dr. Martin Luther King	Mahatma Mohandas Gandhi
Born—when and where?		
Family as a Child		
Parents' Jobs		
College		
Family as an Adult		
Career		
Religion		
Jailed?		
Led Peaceful Demonstrations		
Famous Words		
Died—when and where?		
Remembered For		
After Death		

Stretchy Library Lessons: Multicultural Activities

Men of Peace Answer Key

	Dr. Martin Luther King	Mahatma Mohandas Gandhi
Born—when and where?	Atlanta, Georgia January 15, 1929	Porandar, India October 2, 1869
Family as a Child	sister and brother	one brother
Parents' Jobs	Father—Baptist minister Mother—housewife and teacher	Father—Prime minister in the prince's court (explain this is not a religious position as MLK's father) Mother—housewife
College	Morehouse College, Atlanta, Georgia	College in London, England
Family as an Adult	Married, four children	Married, four children
Career	Minister	Lawyer
Religion	Baptist	Jainism
Jailed?	Yes, for preaching nonviolence, defying unjust American rule and writing anti-segregation pamphlets.	Yes, for preaching nonviolence, defying British rule and writing anti-British pamphlets.
Led Peaceful Demonstrations	Fight prejudice, grant rights to non-whites, eliminate segregation.	Fight prejudice, grant rights to the poor, eliminate British rule.
Famous Words	"I have a dream that my four little children will live in a nation where they will not be judged by the color of their skin but by the content of their character. I have a dream."	"The force of love by peace always wins over violence." "Their suffering is my suffering. The whole world is my family."
Died—when and where?	April 4, 1968, killed by gunshots from assassin.	January 30, 1948, killed by gunshots from an assassin.
Remembered For	Brotherhood for people of all colors, helping to end segregation, advocating nonviolence and love to overcome evil.	Brotherhood for people of all religions, helping to end British rule, advocating nonviolence and love to overcome evil.
After Death	Many streets and buildings named for him, National Holiday established on January 15.	Is called the Father of India.
	Note: MLK went to India in 1959 to learn more about Gandhi's beliefs and actions.	

Immigration

Turning the Tables
(Several Lessons)

Grades: 3–5

Purposes:

- To understand what immigrants encounter in this country.

- To learn something of a country's culture by sharing one of their folktales.

- To learn and share basic facts about selected countries with the class.

- To present a story using props, puppets or a personal rendition.

Prerequisite: Share several of the stories in the resource list with your students. Perhaps show them something of Ellis Island and the Statue of Liberty via the Internet sites listed there as well. Visually and emotionally, students will begin to empathize with the immigrants who have come to the United States from all the countries of the globe. Once that empathy is stimulated, it will be of greater interest for students to research the homelands of their ancestors and the forebears of their classmates.

Format: Research planned with teacher and class presentations. This unit will take several class and/or library periods.

Materials:

- Work in Progress sheet for each child (see page 29)

- letter to parents for each child (see page 30)

- resource materials on various countries from appropriate bookmarked Internet sites, books and reference materials

Prepare in Advance: Plan this unit with the teacher. In my school, students do a continent project each six weeks. One way I contribute is by having a storytelling project students can do in lieu of a written report or research. Pull needed books. Borrow from other schools and the public library if warranted and possible. Gather media and contact speakers, if that is your role on the instructional team. Prepare a handout similar to the example on page 31 for the continent your students are studying.

Activity Directions:

1. A few weeks before the country unit, plan with students what research will be needed. One way to make reference resources go farther is to divide a class into country groups, in which each member is locating different information on the same country. Then a couple of books can meet the needs of the whole group.

2. If students are not familiar with the on-line or computer encyclopedia, plan lessons to instruct them in its use.

3. When students have selected their countries and their areas of interest, show them how to access Yahooligans.com to reach sites that may help them.

4. Set up a schedule in which students can come to the library to work with the computers or reference materials. Plan to assist students as needed.

5. Work with students and teachers, either in the classroom or library, to complete the work in progress form. This will help students focus on their task.

6. When their research is completed, students will present what they have learned to the class according to a schedule arranged with the teacher.

Student Storytelling

Materials:

• puppets and stages from list below

• dashiki

• folktale books (see page 31 for suggestions)

• copies of Asian folktales for each student

• world map to locate countries *(optional)*

Prepare in Advance: Use the professional books in the resource section to learn how to make simple puppets and stages. Teach your students one type of puppet production every six weeks to use for presenting their stories. Demonstrate each type by telling a story yourself. Following is a list of stories I have used with students. Page numbers are from Connie Champlin's book, *Storytelling with Puppets,* or Judy Sierra's book, *Multicultural Folktales.*

Flannel Board Puppet   *(Sierra, pp. 6–8)*
Students draw their puppets on stiff felt or fun foam, cut out and attach a small piece of hook and loop tape to the back. Or they can color and cut out a pattern, mount on poster board and laminate.

Magnetic Board Puppets
Make the same way as you do flannel board puppets, except attach a small piece of magnetic tape to the back. Make your stage from a large steel automotive drip pan covered with felt on one side. Spray paint the backside black and you have an extra large magnetic board.

Overhead Projector Puppets   *(Champlin, pp. 46–48, 186–191)*
These are easy to make because they are silhouettes made from cardboard or plastic. Little artistic talent is needed!

Shadow Stage Puppets   *(Champlin, pp. 46–48)*
Stretch opaque white fabric over a canvas stretcher and tack down. Prop between pairs of bookends, and shine two lights on the backside. Use silhouette puppets attached to flexi-straws. Record your story or have another student read it as you act it out by yourself or with a partner.

Storytelling Without Puppets

I have numerous student-sized dashikis that I loan to students when they tell stories, similar to what an African *griot* would wear to tell stories. Directions for making a very simple dashiki are on page 135 of *Reaching Every Reader* by Pat Miller.

Stick or Finger Puppets in a Box *(Champlin, pp. 25–28, 168–185)*
Stages are made from shoeboxes, cereal boxes and other recycled cardboard boxes.

Hand Puppets on a Stage *(Champlin, pp. 30–42, 216–222)*
Turn a long table on its edge. One student sits on the floor behind it to perform the story while another reads or tells it.

Activity Directions:

1. For the point of this unit, remind students that folktales are passed down by folks orally, and the reason we have so many of them in America is because immigrants and slaves brought the stories with them.

2. The folktale list given here is for Asian folktales. Each week of the six-week period, I tell a cultural story using a different puppetry technique that students can use as a reporting option for their country reports. Select both the story you want to present and the puppetry type you want to demonstrate. These are the ones I use over a school year. Page numbers indicate where patterns are located in my book, *Reaching Every Reader: Promotional Strategies for the Elementary School Library Media Specialist*.

   Overhead Projector Puppetry. *The Blind Men and the Elephant* by Karen Backstein (India)

   Magnetic Board. *Something from Nothing* by Phoebe Gilman (Yiddish) *(pp. 214–215)*

   Flannel Board. *The Bossy Gallito* by Lucia M. González (Cuban) *(see Values lesson in this book, page 38)*

   Shadow Puppetry. *Bony Legs* by Joanna Cole (Russian) *(pp. 208–211)*

   Storytelling. *A Story, A Story* by Gail E. Haley (Ashanti) *(see dashiki directions on p. 135)*

   Stick Puppets. *The Mitten* by Jan Brett (Ukraine) Print masks from Jan Brett's Web site, janbrett.com/mitten_masks_main.htm and attach a tongue depressor to each after mounting and laminating it.

   Hand Puppets on Stage. *Anansi and the Moss-Covered Rock* by Eric Kimmel (Nigeria)

3. Whether they were belowdecks in steerage, crowded together in tenements or slave cabins or simply entertaining their families, people who came to this country shared their tales. The oral tradition is a strong one, not dependent on the ability to read. If possible, begin simply with *A Story, A Story* (Haley), an African tale that explains how all the stories came into the world in the first place. I tell it dressed in a dashiki with a wooden cigar box that is covered with royal purple fabric, sequins and jewels. The box is empty, and I ask the students to guess what such an ornate box must have held. Then I tell them the story of why that treasure box is empty, and about the treasure it once contained.

Resources

Professional Books:

How to Do "The Three Bears" with Two Hands: Performing with Puppets by Walter Minkel. American Library Association, 2000. Includes hundreds of tips for using puppetry in the library program. Scripts are included.

Multicultural Folktales: Stories to Tell Young Children by Judy Sierra and Robert Kaminski. Greenwood, 1991. The first part of the book explains how to tell stories with voice, flannel board and/or puppets. The second contains 25 tales that are grouped by ages two-and-a-half to five, and five to seven. However, I have used the tales with upper grades with much success. Tales include Hispanic, African, European and African American tales. Flannel board patterns are included for each tale.

Reaching Every Reader: Promotional Strategies for the Elementary School Library Media Specialist by Pat Miller. Linworth, 2001. Chapter two is about storytelling and chapter three is about puppetry and how to make and use puppets.

Storytelling with Puppets by Connie Champlin. American Library Association, 1997. Champlin explains everything you need to successfully use puppets. In Part Five, she shows you how to do puppets with book theaters, cups and containers, open-box theaters, overhead shadow stories, panel theaters, stories-in-the-round, story aprons, story totes and tabletop theaters. She includes easy directions for dozens of puppets made from simple materials like paper plates, sacks, socks and tag board.

Books:

Anansi and the Moss-Covered Rock by Eric Kimmel. Holiday House, 1990. (K–3) Anansi is a traditional trickster character. In this book he tricks his friends out of their food until a shy bush deer tricks him.

The Blind Men and the Elephant by Karen Backstein. Scholastic, 1992. (1–3) Six blind men learn about the world through sound and touch. When the prince gets a new elephant, the men decide to go to the palace and touch it. Each man feels only a part of the elephant and gets a different impression of what an elephant looks like. They argue among themselves until the prince tells them that they just need to put all the parts together!

Bony-Legs by Joanna Cole. Scholastic, 1985. (K–3) When a terrible witch vows to eat her for supper, a little girl escapes with the help of a mirror and comb given to her by the witch's cat and dog.

The Bossy Gallito by Lucía M.González. Scholastic, 1994. (K–3) Written in Spanish and English, this is a Cuban folktale of a rooster who dirties his beak on the way to the wedding and asks for help from grass, water, a goat, a stick, a fire, water and his old friend the sun. Reminiscent of the English tale where a farmer is trying to get his pig over the stile to get him home.

Dreaming of America: An Ellis Island Story by Eve Bunting. Troll Communications, 2001. (3–5) Annie Moore, from Ireland, is the first immigrant processed through Ellis Island on January 1, 1892, her fifteenth birthday.

Grandfather's Journey by Allen Say. Houghton Mifflin, 1993. (2–5) Mr. Say's grandfather came to the U.S. as a young man and traveled extensively across it before settling in San Francisco. He returned to Japan for a visit with his wife and daughter. His daughter fell in love and married a Japanese man, and World War II trapped the Say family in Japan. Allen was born in Japan and lived there until he was a teen. The family, minus grandfather who never realized his dream to return to the U.S., moved to San Francisco.

Happy Birthday Mr. Kang by Susan L. Roth. National Geographic Society, 2000. (3–5) Mr. Kang lives in New York City and takes his hua mei bird to the park every Sunday. Both he and his bird are from China, and both have had to make adjustments while missing their homeland. Mr. Kang writes poetry.

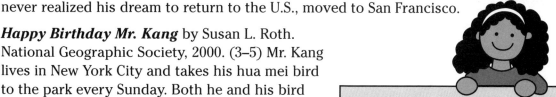

Pair this book with Gollub's *Cool Melons—Turn to Frogs!* (see page 20) and contrast Mr. Kang's poetry with haiku, a Japanese poetry.

The Lotus Seed by Sherry Garland. Harcourt, 1997. (K–5) Share a lotus seed with the class. Bá keeps a lotus seed from the garden of the emperor who was deposed in Vietnam. When her family is driven from their home by war, she comes with them in a small boat to America, where she keeps the seed for hope and remembrance. "No matter how ugly the mud or how long the seed lays dormant, the bloom will be beautiful."

The Mitten: A Ukrainian Folktale by Jan Brett. Putnam, 1989. (K–2) Several animals sleep snugly in Nicki's lost mitten until the bear sneezes.

My Name is Not Gussie by Mikki Machlin. Houghton Mifflin, 1999. (3–5) Golda and her family, Russian Jews, travel to the tenements of New York City in steerage. Hardships and humor are both evident in 14 vignettes of their lives.

Something from Nothing by Phoebe Gilman. Scholastic, 1993. (K–3) Joseph's baby blanket is transformed into ever-smaller items as he grows, until there is nothing left—but then Joseph has an idea.

A Story, A Story by Gail E. Haley. Simon & Schuster, 1976. (K–3) Many African stories, whether or not they are about Kwaku Ananse "the spider man," are called "spider stories." This book is about how they came to be.

The Trip Back Home by Janet S. Wong. Harcourt, 2000. (K–3) The author recalls her childhood trip with her mother to Korea to visit her grandparents and aunt in a small rural village in Korea. Her grandfather dries persimmons on the clay tiles of the roof and sends them back to America as a gift.

Be sure students know what a persimmon is. If possible, bring one in. Follow this story with *The Rabbit's Tail* by Suzanne Crowder Han. It's a funny story about a tiger who is afraid of the unknown dried persimmon and explains why rabbits have short tails.

Two Lands, One Heart: An American Boy's Journey to His Mother's Vietnam by Jeremy Schmidt and Ted Wood. Walker & Company, 1995. (4–5) Phit and her brother and sister are separated from their parents during the flight from the North Vietnamese. Eventually the three children find their way to America where a family in Denver adopts them. When Phit, now called Heather, has children of her own, she begins the search for her parents and eventually finds them. This book is the photo essay of her return to Vietnam with her sister and her oldest son, seven year-old T. J. Beautifully photographed and movingly detailed.

A Very Important Day by Maggie Rugg Herold. William Morrow & Co., 1995. (2–5) Two hundred nineteen people from 32 countries become citizens. Many of their stories are told on each double spread.

Watch the Stars Come Out by Riki Levinson. Penguin USA, 1994. (K–3) A young girl travels with her brother to America and gets her first glimpse of Ellis Island and the Statue of Liberty.

Web sites:

Lower Eastside Tenement Museum
www.wnet.org/tenement
Take a virtual 360° tour of an historic tenement that housed many immigrants in its day. The site explains the conditions of the people who lived there.

The Puppetry Home Page
www.sagecraft.com/puppetry
Sites include Puppetry Traditions Around the World, Puppet Building, Materials, Using Puppetry and more.

U.S. Immigration: 1880–1914
teacher.scholastic.com/researchtools/researchstarters/immigration/
Sites include the Statue of Liberty, Ellis Island, Immigration, Living Conditions for Immigrants, Hull House and much more.

Many of these books tell how long the voyage to America took. Mark a demonstration calendar with an X for each day they are aboard ship, beginning with the date you read the book to the class. Ask students to guess how long the trip would take now. Check by going to an airline's Web site and enter the departure city and New York City.

Work in Progress

Name: _____   Teacher: _____

Country: _____

Group Members: _____

Topic: _____

The questions I want to answer are: _____

_____

_____

The things or people that can help me answer these are: _____

_____

_____

Here's what I found out: _____

_____

_____

_____

_____

_____

_____

_____

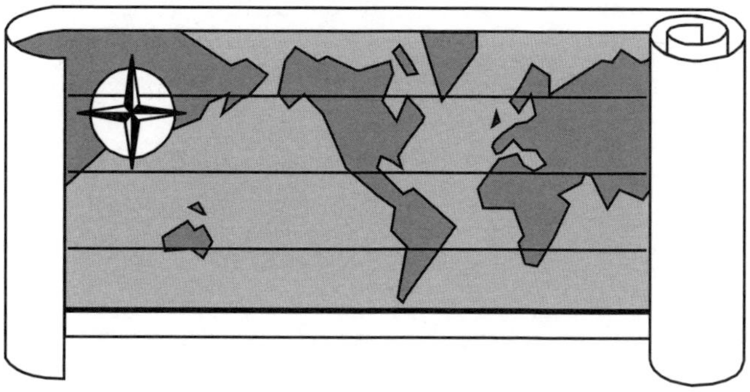

Dear Parents,

We are getting ready to study the people of Asia. Students will be doing research on the customs, geography, foods, games and other interesting topics about one of the countries on this continent.

Here is a list of the countries and mix-and-match topics and projects your child can choose:

Country	Topic	Project
Japan	Foods	Diorama
China	Clothing	Model
Indonesia	Customs	Report
India	Folktales or folk songs	Folktale performance
Philippines	Flag and money	Poem
Russia	Entertainment	Game
Pakistan	Schools	Recipe and food
Vietnam	Animals	Map
Thailand	Houses	Demonstration
Laos	Famous person	Dance
	Holidays	Skit
	Family life	Photographs
Other Asian country:		
_____		
	Other Asian topic:	Other Asian project:
	_____	_____

Country, topic and project idea are to be decided and turned in by _____.

For country information, go to:
www.yahooligans.com/Around_the_World/Countries

For maps, go to:
www.nationalgeographic.com/xpeditions/atlas/index.html

We look forward to "traveling" with your child!

Sincerely,

The Teachers of Grade _____

Asian Folktales

Tell us a folktale! You can learn your story and tell the class, or you can tape the story and use it to accompany your puppet play or shadow play. Or you might want to rewrite it as a Reader's Theater script that your friends can read for the class. Guidelines for scripts are found at Aaron Shepard's Web site: www.aaronshep.com/rt/Tips1.html.

KOREA

The Chinese Mirror / Ginsburg
The Green Frogs / Heo
The Korean Cinderella / Climo
Korean Folktales / Riordan
In the Moonlight Mist / San Souci
The Princess and the Beggar / O'Brien
Rabbit and the Dragon King / San Souci
The Rabbit's Escape / Han
The Rabbit's Tale / Han
Sun and Moon / Seros
Tiger and the Dried Persimmon / Park
A Tiger by the Tale / Curry

PERSIA (IRAN)

*Aladdin and Other Tales from the
    Arabian Nights* / Kerven
Ali Baba and the Forty Thieves / McVitty
The Legend of the Persian Carpet / de Paola
The Persian Cinderella / Climo
Sinbad the Sailor / Sin
The Tale of Aladdin and the Wonderful Lamp /
    Kimmel
Tales from the Arabian Nights / Commager
The Wonderful Bag / Wade

RUSSIA

Baba Yaga / Kimmel
Baboushka / Scholey
Bony Legs / Cole
Clay Boy / Ginsburg
Dancing Bears / Saberhagen
The Fool of the World and the Flying Ship / Ransome
The Gigantic Turnip / Tolstoy
The Golden Sandal / Hickox
Grey Neck / Kronz
Seven Daughters and Seven Sons / Cohen
The Snow Child / Ziefert
Tales of Tricksters / DeSpain
The Turnip / Ziefert

EGYPT

Egyptian Cinderella / Climo
Gift of the Nile / Mike
Heavenly Zoo / Lurie
Popular Stories of Ancient Egypt / Maspero
Rimonah of the Flashing Sword / Kimmel
The Shipwrecked Sailor / Bower
Tales from Africa / Kingfisher
Tales from Ancient Egypt / Hart
Tales of Ancient Egypt / Green
The Winged Cat / Lattimore

INDIA

Anklet for a Princess / Brucher
Blind Men and the Elephant / Backstein
The Cat and the Parrot / Haviland
Jasmine and Coconuts / Spagnoli
The Little Brown Jay / Claire
The Monkey and the Crocodile / Galdone
Once a Mouse / Brown
Rama and Sita / Weitzman
The Rumor / Thornhill
Sanji's Seed / Reinhard
Seven Blind Mice / Young
The Wizard Punchkin / Troughton

JAPAN

The Bee and the Dream / Long
The Boy of the Three-Year Nap / Snyder
The Crane Wife / Bodkin
Funny Little Woman / Mosel
Little Inchkin / French
The Mandarin Ducks / Patterson
Momotaro the Peach Boy / Shute
Peach Boy / Hooks
Sk-Ko and His Eight Wicked Brothers / Bryan
Song of Stars / Birdseye
The Tongue-Cut Sparrow / Ishi

Weather and Seasons

Counting Seasons

MAIN ACTIVITY

Grades: 2–5

Purpose: To learn about alternate ways to mark time through a year.

Format: Read Aloud and Group Interaction

Materials:

- *Moonstick: The Seasons of the Sioux* by Eve Bunting (HarperCollins, 2000)

- chalkboard or overhead projector with blank transparency and pen

- *Moon Tales* by Rina Singh (Bloomsbury Children's Books, 2000)

- Counting Seasons worksheets (see page 35) and pencils

Prepare in Advance: Duplicate enough activity sheets for each pair of students to have one. Each pair will need a pencil.

Activity Directions:

1. Have students list the names of the months in a column on one side of the board or overhead screen. Then have them tell how many days are in each month. Have them list things that happen each month. The list might look like this:

January	31	New Year's Day, snow, cooped up inside school or home all day
February	28/29	Valentine's Day, short month
March	31	spring begins, spring break
April	30	baseball starts, sunny days, play outdoors, Easter
May	31	Memorial Day
June	30	end of school, pools open, barefoot days
July	31	Fourth of July, firecrackers, hot days
August	31	hot summer days, school starts
September	30	Labor Day, back in school, back in shoes
October	31	Halloween, fall leaves color, pumpkins, apples
November	30	Thanksgiving, turkeys, harvest
December	31	Christmas, Hanukkah, Kwanzaa, gifts

In making the list, students might forget the number of days in a month. Tell them that originally, the word month came from moon and the months were 28 days long, the length it takes the moon to go from full moon to "new" and back again. If every month had 28 days we wouldn't have trouble remembering. If they were 28 days, would we still have 12 months in the year? There would be 13 months, which is how the Native Americans kept their calendar. The months were marked on moonsticks and named for what was done or seen that month, just as students described their months.

2. Read aloud *Moonstick,* Eve Bunting's story of a young Sioux coming of age under the 13 moons of the year. Months are named Cherry-Ripening Moon, Moon of the Frost on the Tipi, etc. What do the names of the months have to say about the activities of the Sioux?

3. After reading the book, divide the class into pairs. Give each pair a worksheet and pencil to brainstorm what they would call their assigned month if it were named for its activities. One group can decide when to add the extra month and what it would be called.

4. Teachers could have students use the back of the worksheets to create an illustrated page for each month. Pages could be added to a class book called "The Moonstick Book of _____'s (teacher's name) Class."

5. Follow up this book in succeeding lessons with tales from *Moon Tales* by Rina Singh. The stories are five to eight pages in length, from 10 cultural traditions. You might want to celebrate each new "moon"th, with another legend. (Grades 3–5, younger if read aloud.) Or compare *Seasons of the Sioux* with *An Algonquian Year: The Year According to the Full Moon* by Michael McCurdy.

Seasonal Clothing

Materials:

- Dressing for the Weather worksheets (see page 36) and pencils

- class set of intermediate dictionaries, at least one per pair of students

Prepare in Advance: Reproduce enough copies of the worksheets for students, round up and sharpen enough pencils, gather intermediate dictionaries.

Activity Directions:

1. Distribute pencils and worksheets. Read *The First Rains* by Peter Bonnici. The note on the last page explains what the terms "pump" and "mackintosh" mean. Share the definitions before reading the story.

2. Read over words with students and explain the instructions. Put the words "mackintosh" and "pump" in the correct category with the correct weather. Ask students to complete the rest of the sheet themselves.

3. Use answer key to check answers.

Resources

Books:

An Algonquian Year: The Year According to the Full Moon by Michael McCurdy. Houghton Mifflin, 2000. (2–5) Describes the life of the Algonquian Indians, month by month, as it would have been before the arrival of white settlers.

Dancing Teepees: Poems of American Indian Youth edited by Virginia Driving Hawk Sneve. Holiday House, 1989. (3–5) Poems include topics all children write about, with a distinctive Native American cultural flavor.

The First Rains by Peter Bonnici. Lerner Publishing, 1985. (K–2) First published in England, this brief book shows how an Indian boy waits impatiently for the rains of the monsoon season. The pages are filled with the signs that the storm is coming. Talk about the signs that students have observed when a rain or snowstorm is coming, or a hurricane or tornado. In the back, a note explains some of words that may be unfamiliar to students, including "mac" (mackintosh) and "pump." Use these words to kick off the vocabulary game in the sidebar.

> Arrange students in a circle facing one another. The student who begins must name some kind of clothing that is worn outdoors because of weather conditions. Students who repeat, or who can't think of one, scoot back from the circle. Play continues until there are only five students left. Those five may check out an additional book. You could write the words as suggested in a column for the appropriate kind of weather to assist visual learners.

Hurricane! by Jonathan London. William Morrow & Co., 1998. (K–3) Two boys and their parents pack to escape a hurricane and spend a scary night in a Navy bunker.

> Compare/contrast this book with *The First Rains.*

Moonstick: The Seasons of the Sioux by Eve Bunting. HarperCollins, 2000. (K–3) A young Dakota Indian boy describes the changes that come both in nature and in the life of his people with each new moon of the Sioux year.

Moon Tales: Myths of the Moon from Around the World by Rina Singh. Bloomsbury Children's Books, 2002. (3–6) A spellbinding collection of stories about the moon from around the world.

My Chinatown: One Year in Poems by Kam Mak. HarperCollins, 2001. (2–5) Organized chronologically through the seasons, the free verse poems are filled with emotion and are illustrated by realistic paintings.

Web sites:

Dan's Wild Weather Page
www.wildwildweather.com/

Native American Lore Index
www.ilhawaii.net/~stony/loreindx.html
One hundred and fifty on-line tales from tribes of Turtle Island.

Who Lives on the Moon?
www.netlaputa.ne.jp/~tokyo3/e/
Very brief explanations from numerous countries about whom or what their folktales tell them is living on the moon.

Counting Seasons

The former month of _____

will now be called _____ .

This is what happens in this month: _____

_____

_____

_____

_____

_____

By: _____

_____

_____

Stretchy Library Lessons: Multicultural Activities

Dressing for the Weather

Use a dictionary to look up the clothing items in the list below. What part of your body would you wear the item on? Put each item in the correct column. After each item, write the code that tells what kind of weather you would wear the item in.

If the clothes would cover the top and bottom of your body, like an overcoat, put the name in both columns.

Weather Code:

C = cold   **H** = hot   **R** = rainy   **HC** = worn in hot or cold (like underwear)

Clothing Items:

galoshes	anorak	babushka	sandals	cardigan	camisole
chador	shawl	dashiki	neckerchief	kimono	sombrero
leggings	clogs	windbreaker	stole	earmuffs	pullover
mukluks	turban	tam	kilt	dungarees	slacks
beret	serape	parka	drindl	mackintosh	loafers
trousers	pumps	blouse	hood	long johns	yarmulke

HEAD		TOPS		BOTTOMS		FEET	

Dressing for the Weather
Answer Key

Weather Code:

C = cold   **H** = hot   **R** = rainy   **HC** = worn in hot or cold (like underwear)

Clothing Items:

galoshes	anorak	babushka	sandals	cardigan	camisole
chador	shawl	dashiki	neckerchief	kimono	sombrero
leggings	clogs	windbreaker	stole	earmuffs	pullover
mukluks	turban	tam	kilt	dungarees	slacks
beret	serape	parka	drindl	mackintosh	loafers
trousers	pumps	blouse	hood	long johns	yarmulke

HEAD		TOPS		BOTTOMS		FEET	
babushka	HC	windbreaker	HC	drindl	HC	galoshes	R
hood	C	mackintosh	R	dungarees	HC	loafers	HC
chador	HC	cardigan	C	kilt	HC	mukluks	C
yarmulke	HC	camisole	HC	pullover	C	clogs	H
beret	HC	chador	HC	trousers	HC	sandals	H
sombrero	HC	blouse	HC	long johns	C	pumps	HC/R*
turban	HC	long johns	C	leggings	C		
tam	HC	kimono	HC	slacks	HC		
earmuffs	C	sari	HC	chador	HC		
		dashiki	H	kimono	HC		
		parka	C	sari	HC		
		serape	C	dashiki	H		
		stole	HC				
		shawl	HC				
		neckerchief	H				
		anorak	C				

* In American English, pumps are women's heels. In British English, pumps are overshoes for rain.

Stretchy Library Lessons: Multicultural Activities

Values

Honesty

Grades: K–4

Purposes:

- To demonstrate honesty to students.

- To share instructional stories from other cultures.

Format: Read Aloud, Storytelling

Materials:

- *The Empty Pot* by Demi (Henry Holt & Co., 1996)

- a large pot, preferably a glazed one that looks Chinese

- a Chinese fan, black on one side, flowered on the other

- picture of Chinese children

- a small lacquered folding screen *(optional)*

- a figure to represent the emperor *(optional)*

- world map to locate China

Prepare in Advance: Gather book and materials. If you cannot borrow them from a community member or buy them from a neighboring Asian market, order the fan from Oriental Trading, www.oriental.com. If the fan is not black on the reverse, spray paint it black. Reproduce the picture of Chinese children onto card stock. Color it using bright colors. Laminate and attach a tongue depressor to the center back.

Activity Directions:

1. Learn the story, if desired. I find that it is easier for me to tell the story rather than read it if props need to be manipulated. Before I begin, I show the various props to the class and explain their use. We talk about what lacquer is and why it is applied to wooden articles. I use the screen to define the palace, the figure for the emperor and the picture to represent the thousands of children. Show China on the map.

2. In this story, the emperor is searching for an heir. He calls together all the children and tells them to bring a pot. Show the picture of the children, moving it as if they are running to the palace. The emperor plants a seed in each pot. He tells the children to come back in one year with their result and he will use this to choose the successor to the throne. Ping, who usually has incredible success with growing things, cannot get his seed to grow at all, no matter what he tries. His father assures him that he has tried his best, so Ping returns in shame with his empty pot. The story recounts how each child brings

his or her pot, containing gorgeous flowers. To show this, I slowly open the flowered fan, unfolding the flowers as the children continue to bring their flowers. Then when I say, "But Ping's pot was empty," I flip the fan over to the black side and pause.

3. Continue telling or reading the story to the end. Pause a full minute after to let children absorb the situation and then discuss. Why did the emperor conclude that Ping's empty pot proved his honesty? What did the others do that was dishonest? Why would none of the seeds grow?

4. Can students talk about a time when they or someone they knew proved they were honest?

Perseverance

Materials:

- *The Bossy Gallito* by Lucía M. González (Scholastic, 1994)

- flannel or magnetic board

- story figures (see pages 42–43)

- world map to locate Cuba

Prepare in Advance: Duplicate figures to desired size on card stock. Color and laminate. Attach hook and loop tape or a small magnet to the back of the figures to use in telling the story on a flannel or magnetic board. Locate book and display map.

Activity Directions:

1. Show the class where Cuba is. Cuba is slightly smaller than Pennsylvania. Because of its communist regime, Americans are not allowed to visit or trade with Cuba. Many Cubans are farmers, and the country grows and exports sugar, coffee, citrus fruits and tobacco.

2. This is a cumulative tale in which students are invited to participate. At the back of the book are some of the Spanish words used. Before reading, teach students the words and their pronunciation and meaning. Write the words on the chalkboard or chart tablet for visual learners.

3. Tell the story as you manipulate the flannel board pieces.

4. What would have happened at any point if one of the things had done as El Gallito asked? Why was the sun willing to help? Why do you think each thing was unwilling to help at first? At last?

Resources

Books:

The Bossy Gallito by Lucía M.González. Scholastic. 1994. (K–3) Written in Spanish and English, this is a Cuban folktale of a rooster who dirties his beak on the way to the wedding and asks for help from grass, water, a goat, a stick, a fire, water and his old friend the sun. Reminiscent of the English tale where a farmer is trying to get his pig over the stile to get him home.

Creativity by John Steptoe. Houghton Mifflin, 2003. (3–5; Acceptance, Sharing) Charles is surprised when a new boy named Hector comes to his class from Puerto Rico. Hector has dark skin like Charles but straight hair. They become friends. Charles gives Hector a pair of his "correct" shoes and Hector gives Charles his shirt with the palm trees.

The Empty Pot by Demi. Henry Holt & Co., 1996. (K–3) When Ping admits that he is the only child in China unable to grow a flower from the seeds distributed by the emperor, he is rewarded for his honesty.

Gauchada by C. Drew Lamm. Random House, 2002. (2–5; Kindness) This Argentinian story is based on the expression "to make a gauchada" or to do something kind, something with love, without expecting anything in return.

Just Plain Fancy by Patricia Polacco. Random House, 1994. (K–3; Humility) Naomi Vlecke and her sister Ruth tuck an abandoned egg under one of the laying hens. When it is obvious that the new chick is an exotic bird, the girls become worried. They are Amish, or "plain people," and they have heard of a person in a nearby town who was shunned by her neighbors for dressing too fancy. The girls successfully keep Fancy hidden until the stable raising when Fancy hops onto the clothesline and—to the girls' horror—spreads its gorgeous peacock tail. The oldest woman of the group reassures the girls that the fancy bird is God's handiwork and "that's the way of it."

Reuben and the Quilt by Merle Good. Good Books, 2002. (K–3; Selflessness, Generosity) Reuben is Amish and he helps make the quilt that will be sold to raise money for a sick neighbor. When it is stolen, his father uses an unorthodox Amish technique to get it back.

Save My Rainforest by Monica Zak. Volcano Press, 1996. (2–5; Determination, Perseverance) When he was eight years old, Omar Castillo learned of the Lacandon Rainforest, the only one left in Mexico. He spent three years campaigning to save it. He went by foot and bicycle to the President's palace, and the offices of various state governors to try to organize support for the rainforest and a put stop to its destruction.

Sitti's Secrets by Naomi Shihab Nye. Simon & Schuster, 1997. (2–4; Peacemaking, Sensitivity) Mona's grandmother (Sitti) lives on the other side of the world. As Sitti goes to bed, she says, "Your turn!" because she gets up when Mona goes to bed. When Mona visits her Sitti, she shares many experiences and much love, even though she does not speak the language. The illustrations and evocative text take students to a world most have never known to share the love of a grandmother, which most students know, whether you are eating apricot mish-mish or apple pie. The book includes Mona's letter to the U.S. president for peace.

Snow in Jerusalem by Deborah Da Costa. Albert Whitman, 2001. (2–5; Acceptance, Understanding) A stray cat befriends a boy in the Arab Quarter and another in the Jewish

Quarter of the Old City of Jerusalem. The illustrations show the differences between the four quarters and the story tells of the similarities of two children who love the same cat.

When Bear Stole the Chinook: A Siksika Tale by Harriet Peck Taylor. Farrar, Straus and Giroux, 1997. (2–5; Courage, Teamwork) An orphan boy of the Siksika tribe braves the bitter winter to reclaim the chinook (warm wind that brings spring) from the huge bear that has it trapped in his cave.

Web sites:

Character Education by the Book (Professional)
teacher.scholastic.com/professional/todayschild/charactered.htm
Two teachers explain how they use literature to examine universal values.

Character Education Resources for Students (Professional)
www.bu.edu/education/caec/files/forstudents.htm
Choose the grade level, and find several book titles suggested for the values of citizenship, courage, compassion, diligence, respect, responsibility, self-mastery and truth.

The Bossy Gallito Story Figures

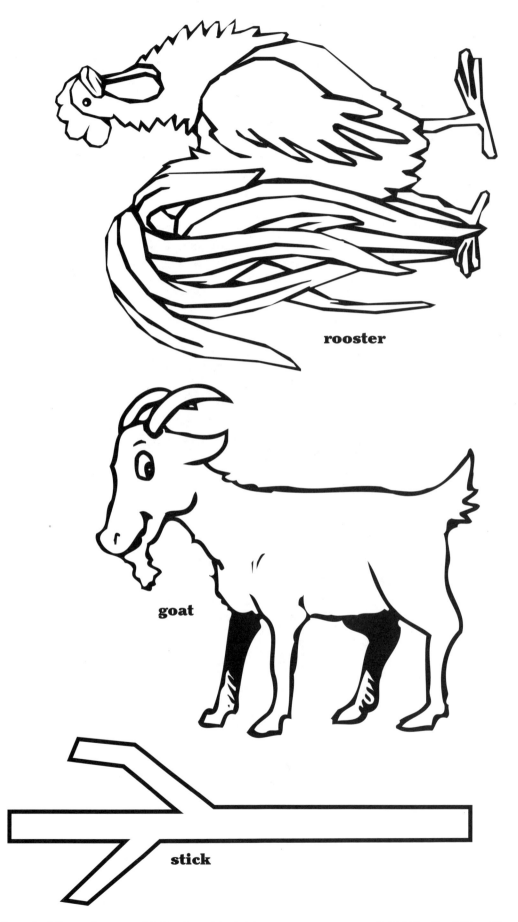

rooster

goat

stick

The Bossy Gallito Story Figures (continued)

sun

fire

grass

puddle

Work and Play

Kids Just Want to Have Fun

Grades: K–2

Purposes:

- To share the universality and differences of play around the world.

- To make students aware that people all over the world have similarities in their emotions, thoughts and behaviors.

Format: Read Aloud, Games

Materials:

- *Come Out and Play* by Maya Ajmera and John D. Ivanho (Charlesbridge Publishing, 2001)

- world map

- Fuku Warai game board and pieces

- game sign for jen-dow, shih-toe, boo

- a scarf for a blindfold

- small paper cup with five kidney beans or buttons for each team of two players *(optional)*

Prepare in Advance: Make a Fuku Warai game board. Fuku Warai is a game played in Japan for the New Year celebration. Fuku means "good fortune." It is played similar to Pin the Tail on the Donkey, but involves building a face. There are two ways to make the game, depending on whether you want permanence or not. For the temporary version, simply draw a large head shape on a chalkboard. For a permanent version, attach a large head shape drawn on paper to a magnetic board. Make small sets of features (eyes, nose, mouth, eyebrows, etc.) and attach magnets to the back of each. Make enough complete sets for an entire class to use. If desired, set a timer and the team with the most features attached when it goes off, gets a point. Then let the next group of players attach their set of features with a new time limit.

Duplicate the jen-dow, shih-toe, boo sign from page 49 so that an entire class can refer to it. On the board or chart tablet, write:

el caballo = horse	el cerdo = pig	two = dos
la cabra = goat	la culebra = snake	three = tres
el perro = dog	el gallo = rooster	four = quatro
la hormiga = ant	one = uno	five = cinco

On the chalkboard, write this phrase in large letters: ¿Mamá, puedo o no puedo? (Mother, may I or may I not?)

Activity Directions:

1. Read aloud *Come Out and Play.* Discuss the pictures that show ways children play around the world. Show locations of some of the countries mentioned on the world map.

2. Have students talk about some of their favorite games relative to what they saw in the picture. Talk about their favorite pastimes in summer and winter. What do they play with a group, with one friend and by themselves?

3. Teach students two simple games from Asia that are similar to ones we play in America.

   Play Jen-dow, Shih-toe and Boo. This game is played the way we play Rock Paper Scissors. Use the Chinese words Jen-dow (scissors), Shih-toe (paper) and Boo (rock). Chant the three words as partners raise their fists up and down to the count. On "Boo," students show their choice of the three. Five fingers stretched out are paper; two are scissors; a clenched fist is the rock. Jen-dow cuts Shih-toe, Shih-toe covers Boo, and Boo breaks Jen-dow. Students can keep score if desired, using five kidney beans or buttons in a cup. Each time a player wins, he or she takes a bean or button. The first player to earn five beans or buttons is the champion.

   Play Fuku Warai. This game is played like Pin the Tail on the Donkey. Draw a large face shape on the chalkboard. Blindfold the first player, and give him/her a piece of chalk. Turn the child three times, and then send him or her a few feet to the board to draw an eye. The next child draws an eye, the next the nose, etc. This will be their "lucky" face and is bound to get your class giggling. For a more permanent version, play with a magnetic board and laminated facial features.

4. If you have more time, play a game from Puerto Rico that resembles "Mother May I." It will help students learn the names of some animals and numbers in Spanish. This game is best played in groups of five, one player is Mamá and four players are the children. Mamá stands at the front of the group, with a large space between her or him and the rest of the players, who are behind a starting line. Mamá begins at one end of the line and chooses a player. She then chooses an animal and the number of steps for the player to take. She would say something like, "Bonnie, take quatro steps like el gallo." Bonnie would answer back, "¿Mamá, puedo o no puedo?" If the player takes a step before asking permission, he or she loses a turn. But if the player remembers, Mamá answers, "Puedes (you may)." Play continues down the line, skipping those who have lost their turns. The first child who gets close enough to tag Mamá becomes the new mother.

Galimoto

S·T·R·E·T·C·H·Y ACTIVITY

Materials:

- *Galimoto* by Karen Lynn Williams (William Morrow & Co., 1990)

- bookmarks for each student (see below)

- a galimoto made from pipe cleaners to use as an attention getter *(optional)*

- world map or map of Africa to locate Malawi

Prepare in Advance: Duplicate the bookmarks below for each student. If there is time, be prepared to demonstrate how to use the Etch-A-Sketch site (www.etch-a-sketch.com/html/on lineetch.htm) to draw a galimoto.

Activity Directions:

1. Locate Malawi in Africa to show students. Locate your hometown. Point out that this story happens on the other side of the Atlantic Ocean.

2. Read aloud *Galimoto.* If you made one, show the class your pipe cleaner galimoto.

3. Tell them they can make one themselves, either from pipe cleaners, or on-line. Show the Etch-A-Sketch site and explain how it is used.

4. Give each student a bookmark featuring the Etch-A-Sketch Web address to take home and extend the lesson.

Draw your own galimoto at this Internet site:

Etch-A-Sketch

www.etch-a-sketch.com/html/onlineetch.htm

Kids around the world just want to have fun!

Resources

Professional Books:

The Multicultural Game Book: More than 70 Traditional Games from 30 Countries by Louise Orlando. Scholastic, 1995.

Books:

Asian Crafts by Judith Hoffman Corwin. Franklin Watts, 1992. (3–5) Learn to make and use Chinese tangrams, Russian nesting dolls, an Indian game called Pachisi and other fun things to play and give as gifts.

Barrio: José's Neighborhood by George Ancona. Harcourt, 1998. (3–5) Beautiful color photographs illustrate the *barrio* (neighborhood) where José lives, plays and goes to school. His school celebrates many multicultural events, and the book ends with the celebration of José's birthday. Day of the Dead, Halloween, shopping, playing soccer and other activities are shown and explained.

Be Boy Buzz by Bell Hooks. Hyperion, 2002. (K–2) Short and vivid descriptions describe the delight of being all boy.

Come Out and Play by Maya Ajmera and John D. Ivanho. Charlesbridge Publishing, 2001. (K–3) Color photographs and text explain how children from 35 countries have fun. While water play may mean running the sprinkler in America, it may mean floating down a stream or paddling the family canoe in another country.

Down Buttermilk Lane by Barbara Mitchell. Boyds Mills Press, 2003. (K–5) Students will travel a bit of the Amish country of Lancaster, Pennsylvania, as they go on the errands of an Amish family. They choose a pattern for a wedding quilt, shop at the Farmers Market, pick walnuts in Mr. Fisher's yard and visit along the way. Pair this book with the nonfiction in the bibliography for an interesting look at an American culture that thrives without electricity.

Galimoto by Karen Lynn Williams. William Morrow & Co., 1990. (1–3) This book, set in Malawi, features a toy vehicle constructed of wire.

Isabela's Ribbons by Satomi Ichikawa. Penguin Putnam, 1995. (K–2) Compare this book about a girl with dozens of ribbons but no one to play Hide and Seek with to the story of *The Rainbow Fish* (Marcus Pfister).

It's Raining Laughter by Nikki Grimes. Dial Books for Young Readers, 1997. (2–4) Myles Pinkney illustrated the book with photos of his children and their friends, who are bursting with the exuberance and pleasures of childhood. The poems talk about running, playing the piano, hating new glasses, teasing, tickling and going to the library. The first poem is about unusual names and concludes that

> *"Whatever I'm called*
> *or may grow up to be,*
> *I'm a work of art now, obviously."*

Let the Games Begin! by Maya Ajmera and Michael J. Regan. Charlesbridge Publishing, 2000. (3–5) In this nonfiction book, the photos and text explain the benefits, obstacles and fun of sports played by children around the world.

Lights on the River by Jane Resh Thomas. Hyperion, 1996. (2–5) Teresa's family are migrant workers who travel to pick crops. This book humanizes the hard work, poor housing conditions and lack of benefits they experience, and how much Teresa misses her grandmother in Mexico.

Look What We've Brought You From Vietnam: Crafts, Games, Recipes, Stories and Other Cultural Activities from New Americans by Phyllis Shalant. Silver Burdett Press, 1988. (2–5) Play "O-Lang" with beans and cups or chase your classmates in a game called "Bite the Carp's Tail." Learn the folktale that explains why monsoons cause so much damage every year. Make moon cakes or act out "Under the Carambola Tree" with the figures and script provided. Other activities, background information and words are included.

Mirette and Bellini Cross Niagara Falls by Emily Arnold McCully. Penguin USA, 2000. (2–4) Mirette (French) and Bellini (Italian) travel to America to walk across Niagara Falls on a wire. They help Jakob, a young Polish orphan, who saves their lives when the high wire is sabotaged.

The Pot that Juan Built by Nancy Andrews-Goebel. Lee & Low Books, 2002. (2–4) This nonfiction book is written for two different reading levels. On the left side of the pages is a cumulative rhyme that explains how Juan Quezada discovered how Mexican Indian pots are made. The right pages contain prose that explains the traditional art technique that is used to make this beautiful pottery.

Saturday at the New You by Barbara E. Barber. Lee & Low Books, 1994. (1–3) Shauna helps out at her mother's beauty parlor, watching all the different customers that come for cuts and sets.

Snake Charmer by Ann Whitehead Nagda. Henry Holt & Co., 2002. (3–5) Vivid color photographs tell of the simple existence of Sher Singh and his family and how they live and play and charm snakes. He has hopes that his son, Vishnu, and his other children will have better lives because they are learning to read and write at their local school. A three-page "About Snake Charmers and Their Snakes" informational section follows and explains how snakes are charmed and why such a life is difficult and poor.

Web site:

Mancala
imagiware.com/mancala
Once students are comfortable playing this strategy game with beans and "pits," send them to the computer to play it two-dimensionally against the computer.

Software:

Strategy Challenges: Around the World, Collection I. Edmark, 1995. Teach problem-solving with these three international games: Nine Men's Morris, Go-Moku and Mancala.

Jen-dow, Shih-toe and Boo

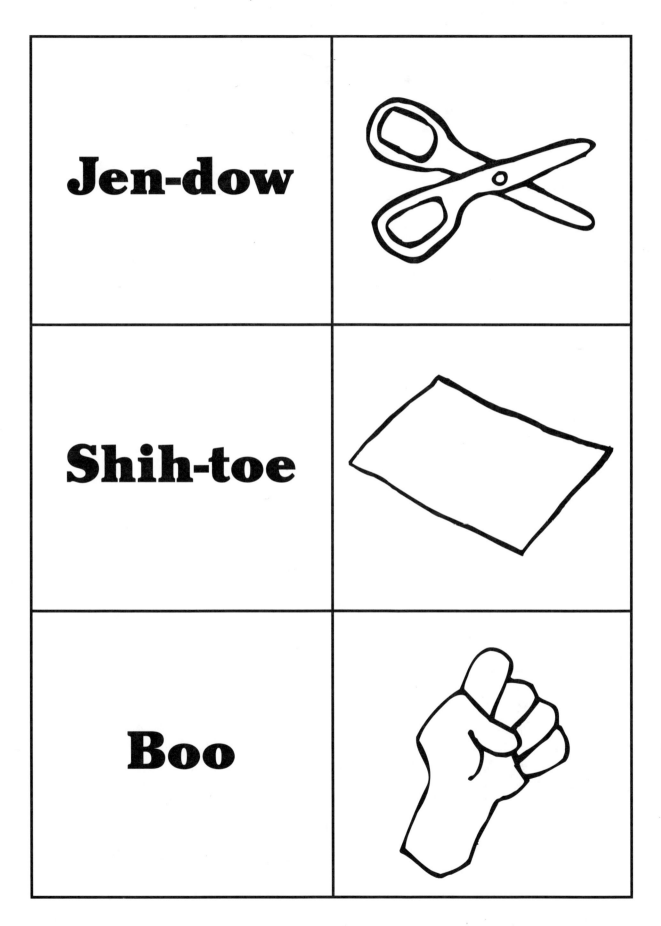

Jen-dow

Shih-toe

Boo

Food

Mama Provi and the Pot of Rice

Grades: K–2

Purposes:

- To learn that like Mama Provi's lunch, life is richer because of the contributions of all ethnic groups.

- To remember the people and their food contributions in sequential order.

Format: Participatory storytelling with flannel or magnetic board.

Materials:

- *Mama Provi and the Pot of Rice* by Sylvia Rosa-Casanova (Simon & Schuster, 2001)

- flannel or magnetic board

- story figures (see pages 54–55)

- small cloth or paper bag with handle (all figures must fit inside)

- a neckerchief or handkerchief, laminated, if using a magnetic board

- a large piece of flannel, colored in checks to look like a tablecloth, if using a flannel board

Prepare in Advance: Duplicate the story figures. Make eight copies of the door. Color and cut out all figures, enlarging if desired. Write a name on each door: Mama Provi, Mrs. Landers, Señor Rivera, Mrs. Bazzini, Mrs. Johnson, Mrs. Woo, Mrs. Kelly and Lucy. Mount the figures on card stock and laminate. Attach a small piece of magnetic tape if using a magnetic board, or a small bit of the hook side of hook and loop tape. Arrange the doors on the board in stair step order as if they are on different floors of an apartment building. Hide the following behind each door: Mama Provi-chicken and rice, Mrs. Landers-bread, Señor Rivera-frijoles négros (black beans), Mrs. Bazzini-fresh green salad, Mrs. Johnson-collard greens, Mrs. Woo-pot of tea and Mrs. Kelly-apple pie.

Activity Directions:

1. Read or tell the story of Mama Provi. When she cooks the chicken and rice, put the pot figure in the bag that Mama Provi carries upstairs. As she shares with each neighbor, open the designated door and put the food item in the sack.

2. Before going to the next door say, "Now let's remember, what's in the bag?" Children should answer in order with the name and the food item. Repeat with each door until you get to Lucy's apartment. Then have a feast using the laminated fabric as a tablecloth. Students should name each item in order before you pull it out and attach to the cloth.

3. For older students, ask how this picnic is like our community.

World of Food

Materials:

- dictionaries

- set of food and country cards (see page 56)

- snack food, preferably one that is linked to a country (e.g., shortbread cookies or gob-stopper candies from England)

- world map to locate countries *(optional)*

Prepare in Advance: Duplicate cards and mount them on two colors of tag board: countries on one color and foods on the other. Laminate and cut them out.

Activity Directions:

1. Distribute cards so that each student has one. If there are extras, give them to students who would like to have two (include the teacher).

2. Put out enough dictionaries for every two children.

3. Tell each child that they will receive a little treat if they can correctly match the country of origin with their food. Give students with food cards time to look up their food item. After a time limit, ask students to close the dictionaries. Those with country cards should line up on one side of the area, foods on another.

4. The first child with a food card says something like, "I have sushi, who has Japanese? (Or "Who has my country?" if the child does not know.)

5. Correct pairs give you their cards, and sit in the "food court." Incorrect answers go to the end of their respective lines. In this way, all should "win" because by process of elimination, all should be matched up correctly by the end of the game.

Answer Key for World of Food

gyros *Turkish*

sauerkraut *German*

moon cake *Korean*

crepe *French*

Kung Pao chicken *Chinese*

sushi *Japanese*

tacos *Mexican*

caviar *Russian*

falafel *Middle Eastern*

matzo ball *Jewish*

curry *Indian*

crumpet *English*

popcorn *American*

feta cheese *Greek*

pasta *Italian*

Resources

Books:

Apple Pie 4th of July by Janet Wong. Harcourt, 2002. (K–3) A young girl's parents own a Chinese market/restaurant and she is disgusted that they keep it open every day but Christmas, even on the Fourth of July. From the store she sees the parade pass by and she knows that no one will want Chinese food on the Fourth of July. "My parents do not understand all American things." At 5:00, people begin to come in for Chinese food, which her parents have made fresh and fragrant. Their neighbor brings an apple pie when she comes to order. When they finally close the store, the girl and her parents climb to the roof and watch the fireworks and eat apple pie.

Fortune cookies can be purchased in bulk from local Asian groceries, or ordered from Oriental Trading Company, www.oriental.com. They make inexpensive treats when the story is over. Before you pass them out, ask how many students recognize them. Most will have a favorite restaurant or food that they like, showing that there is a demand for Chinese, Vietnamese and Japanese food in most communities.

Big Jimmy's Kum Kau Chinese Take Out by Ted Lewin. HarperCollins, 2001. (K–3) The author/illustrator eats three times a week at the Kum Kau Restaurant in Brooklyn. The restaurant menu is shown on the end pages of the book, and the story is a fictionalized one of the owner's son helping out. The book takes the reader behind the scenes to see the fresh ingredients delivered, the food prepared and the napkins folded. Then the customers come for take out and it gets very busy in the kitchen. Lewin's pictures are detailed and full of human drama.

Bread, Bread, Bread and ***Hats, Hats, Hats*** by Ann Morris. William Morrow & Co., 1993. (K–3) Both books contain colorful photographs of bread or hats from around the world, with captions like "skinny bread, fat bread, round flat bread, bread with a hole" or "soft hats, hard hats, sun hats, fun hats." Illustrations cross cultures. For "sun hat" there is a photo of an Egyptian man in a kaffiyeh and floppy hats on American spectators at a wood-chopping contest in Wisconsin. Pages are indexed in the back with the name of the hat or bread, its country of origin and something about its use or how it is made.

Bread is for Eating by David and Phillis Gershator. Henry Holt & Co., 1995. (K–2) Mamita tells her son to think of the wheat seed, "asleep in the ground." Then think of the seed growing, the farmer who tills and harvests, the worker who loads the grain, the miller who grinds it, the storekeeper who sells the flour and the baker. Finally, she says, "Think of the people around the world dreaming of bread" surrounded by a border of breads eaten worldwide. Includes a repetitive Spanish verse (Spanish, English and music at the back).

Pair this book with *Bread, Bread, Bread.*

How My Parents Learned to Eat by Ina Friedman. Houghton Mifflin, 1987. (2–5) Friedman's father, an American sailor, met her mother, a Japanese student, while on leave in Japan. Her father learned to use chopsticks so he could eat with his future wife, and she learned from her uncle to eat with a fork and knife the British way. They were married and moved to the U.S., where they now eat with both.

See *The Story of Chopsticks* on page 53.

Mama Provi and the Pot of Rice by Sylvia Rosa-Casanova. Simon & Schuster, 2001. (K–2) Mama Provi lives on the first floor and her granddaughter lives on the eighth. When Lucy gets chicken pox, Mama Provi makes an enormous pot of pollo con arroz (chicken with rice) and carries it upstairs in a large bag. She stops at each floor to rest, and is captivated by the smells of cooking at each. She trades part of the soup for Mrs. Lander's bread, Señor Rivera's frijoles négros (black beans), Mrs. Bazzini's fresh green salad, Mrs. Johnson's collard greens, Mrs. Woo's pot of tea and Mrs. Kelly's apple pie. When she gets to the last floor, she and Lucy have a delightful picnic.

Something's Happening on Calabash Street: A Story with Thirteen Recipes by Judith Ross Enderle and Stephanie Jacob Gordon. Chronicle Books, 2000. (K–2) People in a diverse neighborhood get together for a street fair and share all kinds of wonderful food.

The Story of Chopsticks by Ying Chang Compestine. Holiday House, 2001. (1–3) An imaginary tale that explains how a boy too impatient to wait for his food to cool invented chopsticks. Author's note explains how chopsticks were really invented, and is followed by a recipe and directions for using chopsticks.

The Story of Noodles by Ying Chang Compestine. Holiday House, 2002. (1–3) Three mischievous Chinese brothers take a shortcut in their mother's dumpling recipe and end up inventing noodles. Funny pictures show all the ways one can eat noodles.

Strudel Stories by Joanne Rocklin. Random House, 2000. (2–5) Several generations of a Jewish family tell stories while making apple strudel together.

The Tortilla Factory by Gary Paulsen. Harcourt, 1998. (K–2) In just 136 words, Paulsen explains the cycle of planting corn in the rich black earth, harvesting it, grinding it and making it into tortillas that feed the workers that plant the corn in the rich black earth. Paulsen's wife illustrated the book in oil on linen.

> Serve quartered tortilla and jelly or cheese "sandwiches" after reading the story to your students.

Web sites:

Fruit Game
www.2020tech.com/fruit

Pita Bread
teacher.scholastic.com/lessonrepro/lessonplans/ect/pitabr.htm
A simple recipe to send home on how to make this Greek bread.

Plastic Fork Diaries: Food Field Trips
www.plasticforkdiaries.org/fieldtrip/index.cfm
Go behind the scenes at unusual places where food is grown and prepared: a pumpkin farm, a chocolate factory, a bakery, even a school cafeteria.

Mama Provi and the Pot of Rice
Patterns

chicken and rice

loaf of bread

black beans

lettuce and tomato salad

pot of tea

collard greens

apple pie

door

World of Food Cards

sushi	caviar	popcorn
ITALIAN	GREEK	FRENCH
gyros	falafel	pasta
GERMAN	INDIAN	MEXICAN
curry	crepe	sauerkraut
ENGLISH	JEWISH	KOREAN
feta cheese	tacos	crumpet
JAPANESE	CHINESE	AMERICAN
matzo ball	moon cake	Kung Pao chicken
TURKISH	MIDDLE EASTERN	RUSSIAN

Folktales

The Squeaky Door

Grades: K–2

Purposes:

- To learn some Spanish while joining in the refrain and cumulative tale.

- To involve the students in participation with the storytelling.

Format: Storytelling with flannel or magnetic board.

Materials:

- *The Squeaky Door* by Laura Simms (Crown, 1991)

- flannel or magnetic board

- flannel board figures (see pages 61–63)

- map that shows Puerto Rico and the place where your students live

Prepare in Advance: Have a Spanish speaker teach you the few Spanish words so you can say them as accurately as possible. Reread the story numerous times until you can tell it from memory, or practice reading it aloud to fit in the Spanish words.

Cut out the patterns and trace them onto stiff felt or fun foam. Or color and cut out the figures, glue them to card stock and laminate. Make the bed large enough that all characters can fit underneath. Attach a small magnetic strip or the grabby side of hook-and-loop tape to the back. Write "¡Usted me está haciendo loco!" (You are making me crazy!) on a large strip of poster board, or use the card provided (or use the sign on page 62).

Activity Directions:

1. Show the students Puerto Rico on the map. Show where the students live. How would you get to Puerto Rico from here?

2. As you tell the story, act it out on the storyboard. When I tell it, I say, "she tucked him in" (act out pulling up the covers), "kissed him goodnight" (make a loud smacking sound), "and turned off the light" (make the motion of turning off a switch and say "click"). Then move your lower arm as if it is a door swinging shut as you say, "Then Abuela closed the squeaky door." Make the squeakiest sound you can and encourage children to join in with all the above motions and sounds, which repeat throughout the story.

3. When you name the animal that gets frightened and hides under the bed, make the animal's sound effect as you place its figure "under the bed." When Abuela comes back into the room, be sure to click on the light!

Cruise to Puerto Rico  S·T·R·E·T·C·H·Y ACTIVITY

Materials:

- *Children of Puerto Rico* by Michael Elshon Ross (Lerner Publishing, 2001)

- overhead projector and screen

- Puerto Rico cruise game board (see page 65)

- Cruising to Puerto Rico questions sheet (see page 64)

Prepare in Advance: Reproduce the game board on page 65 on a transparency. Use the transparency to enlarge the image on your chalkboard and trace. For a permanent game board, trace onto poster board or a shower curtain liner. Use scraps of laminating film to make pockets that are open on the side. Attach pockets to each destination. (If you are using the chalkboard, write A or B at each port as the teams arrive at port.) Photocopy a cruise ship game piece (see below) in a different color for each team. You may need to enlarge or reduce the game piece to fit the board. Insert the team's cruise ship into the pocket at each destination if the team answers correctly. The first team to cruise to Puerto Rico wins.

Students will need to see the questions and answer choices because they won't remember them if they are just read orally (especially if the question is a rebound). Reproduce questions on a transparency that can be shown next to the game board.

Activity Directions:

1. Divide the class into two teams. Each team has a cruise ship. Teams should sit close together so they can huddle and decide on a team answer. When the team has discussed the answer and all agree, all should raise their hands. When all of the hands are up, call on a student to answer for the team. I like to play this way because it includes all children, and if a student answers incorrectly, it was the team answer, so there are no hard feelings.

2. If the team answers correctly, their cruise ship advances one port. If they are incorrect, the question rebounds to the second team. True/false questions do not rebound. The second team can take the rebound if they answer correctly, but the question will not be reread, nor its incorrect answer repeated. If the rebound is correctly answered, the team gets a bonus port, and then gets to answer the next question as well.

3. The first team to cruise into the port of San Juan, Puerto Rico, is the winner.

cruise ship game piece pattern

Cruising to Puerto Rico Answer Key:

1. True; 2. True; 3. C; 4. True (It's a commonwealth territory); 5. D; 6. A; 7. C and D; 8. B; 9. A; 10. C; 11. A; 12. C; 13. D; 14. B; 15. A

Resources

Professional Books:

Reaching Every Reader: Promotional Strategies for the Elementary School Library Media Specialist by Pat Miller. Linworth, 2001. Includes 12 units that each contain 10 center activities designed to accommodate the multiple intelligences. Three of the units are *Something from Nothing* (includes flannel board figures), *The Mitten* (plus animal research), *Anansi and the Moss-Covered Rock* (with easy directions for making a dashiki for you or your students).

Books:

Aladdin: And Other Tales from the Arabian Nights by Rosalind Kerven. Dorling Kindersley, 2000. (2–4) This is one of the Arabian tales of a poor Chinese boy who retrieves a magic lamp and frees the genie who grants him three wishes. This version includes sidebars with explanations and photos to explain things that students may be unfamiliar with, like incense or genie. The pictures clearly show the Chinese and Persian influences in the story.

Ali Baba and the Forty Thieves by Walter McVitty. Harry N. Abrams, 1989. (4–5) Ali Baba and his dangerous dealings with the thieves is the most popular of the many tales of *The Thousand and One Nights*. The illustrations are done in the style of Persian miniatures from the tenth century and are enhanced with shiny gold.

Anansi and the Moss-Covered Rock by Eric Kimmel. Holiday House, 1990. (K–4) Anansi is a traditional trickster character. In this book he tricks his friends out of their food until a shy bush deer tricks him.

Blue Willow by Pam Conrad. Penguin Putnam, 1999. (4–5) I became interested in this Chinese legend when I received a place setting of the Blue Willow as a dividend at a local grocery store. The blue willow design is fascinating, even more so when one knows the legend of a love that won't be denied, a legend that Pam Conrad adapts for modern readers.

Children of Puerto Rico by Michael Elshon Ross. Lerner Publishing, 2001. (3–5) This excellent resource shows children of various ethnicities involved in typical activities. Students are diverse and include handicapped and those from cities, towns, the country and a university.

The Funny Little Woman by Arlene Mosel. Penguin Putnam, 1977. (K–2). Caldecott Medal Winner. A giggly little woman chases a runaway dumpling underground to the home of the wicked oni where she's captured to become their cook. She takes their magic rice paddle and escapes home, where the paddle helps her to become rich.

Juan Bobo: Four Folktales from Puerto Rico (An I Can Read Book) by Carmen T. Bernier-Grand. HarperCollins, 1995. (K–2) Silly Juan Bobo and his long-suffering mother will have your young listeners giggling. He dresses the family pig for church, "sells" his mama's syrup to flies, goes home hungry from a neighbor's because he tried to obey his mother and carries water home in baskets because the buckets are so heavy. The tales are followed by the Spanish translation.

Momotaro the Peach Boy: A Traditional Japanese Tale by Linda Shute. HarperCollins, 1986. (1–4) Ancient Japanese folktale in which a boy born from a peach gives his mother's rice dumplings to a dog, a monkey and a pheasant, who help him overcome the onis.

Pair this with *The Funny Little Woman.* Both stories tell very different events that surround rice dumplings.

The Monkey and the Crocodile: A Jakata Tale from India by Paul Galdone. Houghton Mifflin, 1997. (K–5) In this short folktale, both monkey and crocodile use their cunning to try to outwit the other. Monkey gets into a jam twice in the story, and uses his wits to escape. Before you read the monkey's solution, ask students what they would do to escape if they were Monkey.

The Princess and the Beggar: A Korean Folktale by Ann Sibley O'Brien. Scholastic, 1992. (3–5) The youngest daughter of the King of Pyung-yang is banished to the cave of the wild mad man, Pabo Ondal, when she refuses to marry the man the king chooses for her. Eventually Pabo Ondal and she become good friends and partners, and she teaches him to read and write. He wins the king's hunting contest and the king's poetry contest, thanks to his wife the princess, and both are invited to come to court.

Shake It, Morena! And Other Folklore from Puerto Rico by Carmen T. Bernier-Grand. Millbrook Press, 2002. (K–5) Use these games and rhymes with many topics. Use the countries/flags game after having introduced many cultures with their maps and flags.

Sky Legends of Vietnam by Lynette Dyer Vuong. HarperCollins, 1993. (4–5) Six tales ranging from the three-page "Why the Rooster Crows at Sunrise" to 23-page "The Seven Weavers." Followed by author's notes and pronunciation key of Vietnamese names.

The Squeaky Door by Laura Simms. Crown, 1991. In this cumulative story, a little boy overcomes his fear of the squeaky noise his door makes when his grandmother closes it each night before he goes to sleep.

The Tale of Rabbit and Coyote by Tony Johnston. Putnam, 1998. (K–3) While many folks think they see a man in the shadows of the moon, a Mexican folktale says it is a rabbit. This is the story of all the ways rabbit tricked coyote and ended up on the moon.

Web sites:

Deep in the Bush Where People Rarely Ever Go
www.phillipmartin.info/liberia/

Folktales on the Web: Internet Field Trip
teacher.scholastic.com/fieldtrp/childlit/folk.htm
There are a variety of activities and sites here, including a unit on how to write folktales by Alma Flor Ada, and how to convert folktales into Reader's Theater scripts by Aaron Shepard.

The Squeaky Door Patterns

Abuela

el niño

el perro

el gato

Stretchy Library Lessons: Multicultural Activities **61**

el caballo

el cerdo

la culebra

"¡Usted me está haciendo loco!"

bed

Cruising to Puerto Rico Questions

1. True or False: Christopher Columbus arrived in Puerto Rico in 1493 and thought he was in India.

2. True or False: Africans were brought to Puerto Rico as slaves.

3. The Taino Indians were in Puerto Rico first. Which of these words is NOT a Taino word?

    a. canoe   b. barbecue   c. surfing   d. hurricane

4. True or False: Puerto Rico is a part of the United States.

5. Which of these is **not** grown in Puerto Rico?

    a. coffee   b. sugar   c. bananas   d. sweet potatoes

6. If you lived in Puerto Rico, which would be a sport you would **not** play?

    a. boat racing   b. softball   c. baseball   d. golf

7. Which two of these dances began in Puerto Rico? (Go to other team for second answer.)

    a. cha cha   b. tango   c. meringue   d. salsa

8. Before it was part of the United States, which country owned Puerto Rico?

    a. Cuba   b. Spain   c. Mexico   d. Brazil

9. What is a coqui?

    a. a small frog   b. a small coconut   c. a type of drum   d. a popular drink

10. Which of the following is not found on Puerto Rico?

    a. tall mountains   b. a rainforest   c. a desert   d. 2,000-year-old trees

11. The capital of Puerto Rico is ___.

    a. San Juan   b. San José   c. San Diego   d. Santa Barbara

12. In which ocean is Puerto Rico located?

    a. Atlantic   b. Pacific   c. Caribbean   d. Mediterranean

13. Which country is closest to Puerto Rico?

    a. Mexico   b. United States   c. Brazil   d. Cuba

14. What kind of money do the Puerto Ricans use?

    a. Mexican pesos   b. dollars   c. Spanish pesos   d. reales

15. What does "Puerto Rico" mean?

    a. rich port   b. open door   c. beautiful island   d. poor and rich

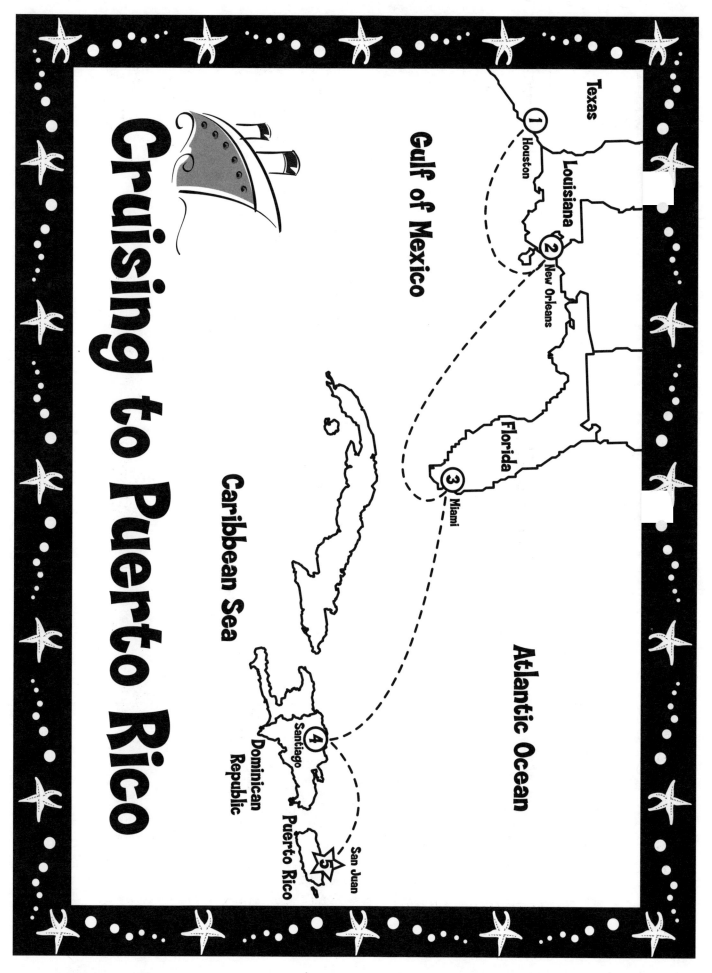

Cruising to Puerto Rico

Texas

1 Houston

Gulf of Mexico

Louisiana

2 New Orleans

Florida

3 Miami

Atlantic Ocean

Caribbean Sea

4 Santiago

Dominican Republic

Puerto Rico

San Juan

5

Celebration

Chinese New Year

MAIN ACTIVITY

Grades: 3–5

Purposes:

- To learn some traditions and a legend from China.

- To look at measurement of time from another perspective.

- To retell story a using Reader's Theater.

Format: Discussion and Demonstration, Reader's Theater

Materials:

- bookmark with Chinese characters

- world map or globe to locate China

- *Cat and Rat: The Legend of the Chinese Zodiac* by Ed Young Henry Holt & Co., 1998)

- copy of Chinese Zodiac for each student or teacher, printed from the Internet

Prepare in Advance: Photocopy the bookmark below for each student. Run four of them on a sheet of red paper. Cut them apart. The dot indicates the top of bookmark. If desired, punch a hole through the dot and tie with a red ribbon. Print the Chinese Zodiac from the "Discovering China" Internet site (page 68) to have on hand for explaining the characteristics of each animal in the Chinese Zodiac. You may want to make a copy for each teacher to share with students.

Gung Hay Fat Choy 浪漫哪茶 .

Activity Directions:

1. Locate China on a map. Also point out Vietnam, which celebrates a New Year holiday called Tet. Tet lasts for three days, and falls at the same time as the Chinese New Year. The Vietnamese also give animal names to their years, though the list of animals is slightly different. The Vietnamese Zodiac includes: mouse, water buffalo, tiger, cat, dragon, snake, horse, goat, monkey, chicken, dog and pig. See Step 3 for the list of Chinese animals.

2. Explain to students that this year in the Chinese calendar will be _____ (the year 2004 is 4702). Why do you think there is such a discrepancy between their calendar and the one we use? (One reason is because the Chinese calendar is based on the moon, making all the months 28 days long. The other is that unlike the Gregorian calendar used in the West, the Chinese did not divide history at the birth of Christ, but kept counting.)

3. While the Western calendar counts by tens or decades, the Chinese calendar marks years in dozens. The years are named for 12 animals, and people born during that year are thought to have the qualities of that animal. The twelve animals of the Chinese Zodiac, in order, are: rat, water buffalo, tiger, rabbit, dragon, snake, horse, goat, monkey, rooster, dog and pig. The year 2003 is the year of the goat. See Internet sites on page 68 for more information.

4. Read aloud *Cat and Rat: The Legend of the Chinese Zodiac* by Ed Young. It retells the Chinese legend explaining why rat is first and why many beloved animals are missing from the calendar. If time allows, perform the Cat and Rat Reader's Theater.

5. Give students the bookmark that says Happy New Year. It is pronounced "Gung hay fat choy."

Cat and Rat Reader's Theater

Materials:

- scripts for 18–20 readers, plus one for teacher and one for you

Prepare in Advance: Make 22 copies of the script that follows. On each copy, highlight an animal name, then all of its lines. Do the same for each copy, highlighting a different character.

Note: You can split the parts of the cat and rat at the asterisk to allow two more students to participate. Mark their scripts appropriately.

Activity Directions:

1. Ask readers to read their parts aloud softly to themselves while their classmates check out books. You or the teacher should be on hand to help with unfamiliar words.

2. Have students line up in zodiac order, with the rat first and the pig last. Designate a finish line and the river. The Emperor stands on the far side of the river. You or the teacher sit where you can prompt students if needed.

3. Perform the script by reading the parts. Students move across the finish line as indicated in the script.

4. If two readers are chosen for the parts of cat and rat, inform the audience that there will be a change of readers, but not characters, for cat and rat.

5. You may want to make headbands for the readers so the audience can remember who is who. Cut an 18" strip of construction paper for each headband. Glue a character's picture or narrator nameplate from pages 73–76 to the center of each headband. Laminate for durability. Wrap the headband to fit the child's head and staple.

Sample Character Headband

Resources

Books:

Cat and Rat: The Legend of the Chinese Zodiac by Ed Young. Henry Holt & Co., 1998. (K–3) Introduces the Chinese Zodiac and relates how each of its 12 signs was named for an animal selected by the Jade Emperor.

Celebrating Chinese New Year by Diane Hoyt-Goldsmith. Holiday House, 1998. (3–5) Depicts a San Francisco boy and his family preparing for and enjoying their celebration of the Chinese New Year, their most important holiday.

Lion Dancer: Ernie Wan's Chinese New Year by Kate Waters. Scholastic, 1990. (K–3) Describes six-year-old Ernie Wan's preparations, at home and in school, for the Chinese New Year celebrations and his first public performance of the lion dance.

Sam and the Lucky Money by Karen Chinn. Lee & Low Books, 1995. (2–4) Share the excitement of Chinese New Year in Chinatown, complete with the sights, sounds and smells of this noisy and festive holiday. This story will touch the hearts of readers as Sam becomes aware of the needs of others.

Web sites:

Chinese New Year
www.educ.uvic.ca/faculty/mroth/438/CHINA/chinese_new_year.html
Includes sites for the 15-day celebration of Chinese New Year, traditional New Year foods, decorations, taboos and superstitions of the New Year.

Discovering China
zone.cps.k12.il.us/Showcase/Student_Projects/China/china.html
Build and fly kites, learn about Chinese food and the Great Wall, count in Chinese, read about pandas and learn about Chinese accomplishments. Type in your birth date and discover your traditional Chinese sign, personal qualities and the most compatible signs.

Reader's Theater Script
Cat and Rat

by Pat Miller
Adapted from *Cat and Rat: The Legend of the Chinese Zodiac* by Ed Young.
Henry Holt & Co., 1995. © 1995 by Ed Young.

Readers: Emperor; Rat (2); Cat (2); Rabbit; Tiger; Dog; Goat; Snake; Dragon; Water Buffalo; Pig; Horse; Rooster; Narrator 1; Narrator 2; Narrator 3; Narrator 4

Emperor: I will honor the twelve best animals in China by naming a year for each of them. We will have a race.

Narrator 1: The Emperor set a racecourse through the thickest part of the forest and across the widest point of the river.

Cat: Rat, wouldn't it be wonderful to have years named for such good friends as you and me?

Rat: Cat, you are my best friend. But we are the smallest animals. We'll never beat the bigger, faster animals.

Cat: I have an idea.

Narrator 2: The cat took the rat to see Water Buffalo.

Cat: Water Buffalo, are you going to be in the Emperor's race?

Water Buffalo:
Yes. I plan to get up before the sun to get a head start.

Cat: Would you mind if we keep you company by riding on your back?

Water Buffalo:
I would like your company. Sleep near me tonight so we can be ready early.

Narrator 3: In a few short hours, while it was still dark, Water Buffalo woke Rat and Cat.

Rat: I can't believe you got me up so early!

Water Buffalo:
It's time. We must start now if we want to win the Emperor's race.

Narrator 4: Cat and Rat climbed on his back. They fell fast asleep as Water Buffalo trotted through the thick forest.

Cat: Rat, wake up! We are already entering the river.

Rat: I can see the Emperor waiting on the far side of the river.

Narrator 1: Now Rat began to think about the honor of being first.

Narrator 2: Rat was selfish and decided he wanted the honor for himself.

*Rat 2: My friend, look! The river is filled with delicious fish!

Narrator 3: When Cat leaned over Water Buffalo's hip to look, Rat pushed her off.

Cat: Help me, Rat! I hate water. Stop, Water Buffalo!

Narrator 4: Water Buffalo turned his head towards Cat, but he saw that the other animals were not far behind.

Water Buffalo:
Cat, I cannot go back for you. Swim to that log instead.

Narrator 1: Just as Water Buffalo's hooves touched the riverbank, Rat jumped from his head and scampered across the finish line.

Emperor: I am surprised to see you, Rat. How does it happen that one so small should be first?

Rat 2: I'm small but I'm smart.

Water Buffalo:
You tricked me, Rat. I did all the walking and swimming but have to be second. I am sorry that I helped you.

Narrator 2: Meanwhile, Cat struggled to reach the floating log. Tiger swam close by.

Tiger: I hate being wet as well, Cat. But the faster I swim, the sooner I can get out.

Narrator 3: Tiger crawled out of the water and ran across the finish line.

Tiger: Am I first?

Rat 2: No. You are not clever enough to beat me.

Water Buffalo:
You have to wake up very early to beat me.

Emperor: You are third, Tiger.

Narrator 4: A huge storm darkened the sky and lightning flashed. Dragon was seen flying through the flashing light.

Dragon:	I am too big to run the forest or swim the river. The Emperor gave me permission to fly through the dangerous storm instead.
Rabbit:	I cannot fly, but I can run fast. I will not rest until I cross the finish line.
Narrator 1:	Just as Dragon was coming in to land, Rabbit hopped across the finish line.
Emperor:	Well done, Rabbit. You are fourth. Dragon, you are fifth.
Cat:	This log is floating past the Emperor. I will have to jump back into the river.
Narrator 2:	As cat jumped, he landed in the water near Snake.
Snake:	Get out of my way, Cat, or I will bite you.
Cat:	Be careful, Snake. You're pushing me under!
Snake:	Move aside. I will have the honor of a year.
Narrator 2:	The snake slithered across the finish line in sixth place.
*Cat 2:	I can't see. There is water in my eyes.
Narrator 3:	A wave washed Cat to the side as horse swam by.
Horse:	I hope you can see me coming. I have run as fast as I can. Move aside.
Narrator 4:	Horse splashed past Cat and came in seventh. As soon as Horse left the water, Goat and Monkey could be heard arguing.
Goat:	Out of my way, Monkey. You don't deserve a year named for you.
Monkey:	Let go of my tail. You don't deserve a year even more.
Narrator 1:	Goat and Monkey fought in the water, keeping Cat from the riverbank. They rushed from the water.
Goat:	I win!
Monkey:	I win!
Emperor:	BOTH of you win. Goat, you are eighth and Monkey, you are ninth.
Cat 2:	Even Rooster is swimming better than I am.
Rooster:	It helps to have wings to flap when you swim.
Narrator 2:	Close behind Rooster, Dog was dog paddling.

Dog: I love water. This is so fun that I could play all day!

Cat 2: I hope you do. I don't want to be last.

Narrator 3: Dog played for several minutes, but paddled to the edge when he saw Rooster leaving the water.

Rooster: I made it. Hurray for me! Hurray for me!

Emperor: Stop crowing for yourself, Rooster. It is enough that you will have the tenth year.

Dog: Wasn't that swimming the most fun ever?

Emperor: I'm glad you had fun. You will also enjoy having the eleventh year.

Cat 2: I think I have swallowed half this river. Only a few more feet to go.

Narrator 2: Just then, Pig came oinking and splashing.

Pig: No one thought I could win, but watch me go!

Cat 2: Wait, Pig. Wait for me.

Pig: Sorry, Cat. Maybe if I win, I won't be laughed at so much.

Narrator 4: Pig rushed past the Emperor. He was named the twelfth and final winner. Still the Cat did not give up.

Narrator 1: Finally Cat reached the edge of the river and dragged herself up the bank.

Cat 2: Please Emperor; tell me it's not too late.

Emperor: I am proud of your courage, dear Cat. But I'm afraid that the twelve places have been filled.

Cat 2: Rat, you betrayed me!

Narrator 2: Cat screamed in anger and leaped at the rat.

Narrator 3: Her claws scratched Rat's tail, but he escaped under the throne of the Emperor.

Narrator 4: And that is why, to this day, Cat is the enemy of Rat.

The End

Cat and Rat Patterns

Emperor

Rat

Cat

Water Buffalo

Tiger

Pig

Rabbit

Dragon

Cat and Rat Patterns (continued)

Dog

Monkey

Goat

Horse

Rooster

Snake

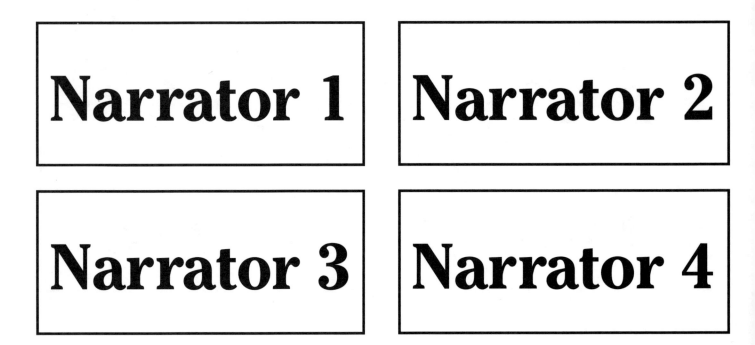

Narrator 1	Narrator 2
Narrator 3	Narrator 4

Additional Resources

A search of your library catalog and public library catalog will yield a rich crop of multicultural materials. Following are some additional sites and books I have read and used with my students:

AFRICA

Africa Brainteaser Quiz
www.nationalgeographic.com/ngkids/games/brainteaser/brain.html
Eight multiple-choice questions like "How many countries are in Africa?" Correct answers get more information. Incorrect choices bring up the correct answer.

The Village of Round and Square Houses by Ann Grifalconi. Little, Brown and Company, 1986. (3–5) The author tells about life in the villages she visited in the Cameroon.

AMISH

American Quilt Making: Stories in Cloth by Ann Stalcup. Rosen Publishing Group, 2003. (3–5) Includes double page spreads about African American, Amish, AIDS, album, friendship, Hawaiian, Hmong and picture quilts.

The Amish by Doris Faber. Doubleday & Co., 1991. (4–5)

Amish Home by Raymond Bial. Houghton Mifflin, 1993. (3–5)

Amish Photo Gallery
www.amishphoto.com/galleryindex.htm (all ages)

The Amish and the Plain People
www.800padutch.com/amish.shtml (3–5)

An Amish Year by Richard Ammon. Atheneum, 2000. (3–5)

Growing Up Amish by Richard Ammon. Atheneum, 1989. (4–5)

CHINA

Look What Came from China by Miles Harvey, Scholastic Library Publishing, 1999. (2–5) Includes information about food, tools, toys, crafts, musical instruments, fashion, sports and more. Share this book before celebrating Chinese New Year, or before sharing other books listed in this bibliography.

Did you know?
The Chinese invented the earliest kind of computer called an abacus, as well as paper, printing and fireworks. Rice, tea and soybeans are foods popularized by the Chinese thousands of years ago, and are still eaten in many countries around the world. They invented ice cream and pasta, the compass, saddle and wheelbarrow, kites, dominoes and the foot game we call hacky sack in the United States. They also invented calligraphy, a beautiful way of writing with pen and black ink.

INDIA

Chanda and the Mirror of Moonlight by Margaret Bateson-Hill. Zero to Ten Limited, 2001. (3–5) If you can find fabric from India that is embroidered with tiny mirrors, you will have an excellent visual to accompany this story of a poor girl named Chanda. She is kidnapped on her wedding day so her wicked stepsister can marry the prince in her place. A peacock, a broken mirror and Chanda's delicate sewing skills help to reunite her to her prince, and give fictional rise to the mirrored fabric of India.

Let's Investigate Nations: India by Adele Richardson. The Creative Company, 2000. (3–5) Use some of the photos and facts from this book to interest students in further research. For example, two games that were invented in India are polo and badminton, both of which were learned by the British and taken back to England and renamed. Surprisingly, this book has no map, so be prepared to have one ready to point out the sights mentioned in the text.

JAPAN

Kids Web Japan
jin.jcic.or.jp/kidsweb/index.html
Experience the Japanese culture virtually, by moving flowers into a vase to learn Ikebana, finding directions for Origami, trying to write Japanese letters with a brush in Shodo, play a traditional Japanese tune on a Koto and much, much more in this interesting, kid-friendly site.

KOREA

Count Your Way Through Korea by Jim Haskins. Lerner Publishing, 1988. (2–5) Students learn brief facts about Korea, like the fact that they traditionally use eight spices in their meals, which are spicier than most Asian meals, and that they won the twenty-seventh World Baseball Championship the same year the first Korean professional baseball league was formed.

The Korean Cinderella by Shirley Climo. HarperCollins, 1993. (K–3)

The Rabbit's Tail: A Story from Korea by Suzanne Crowder Han. Henry Holt & Co., 1999. (K–3) Rabbit outsmarts Tiger by preying on his fear of the unknown.

MEXICO

Look What Came From Mexico by Miles Harvey. Scholastic Library Publishing, 1998. (2–5) Contributions are grouped by food, fashion, inventions, music, toys, animals, words, festivals and more. Inspire interest by asking these questions before reading. Do not answer them, but let the children hear the answers as you read.

Which of the following foods was not first cultivated or made in Mexico?
(Answers: Tea and beans)

squash	chili peppers	corn	tea	tamales
tortillas	tacos	beans	chocolate	

True/False. The following were invented in Mexico:
(false: baseball, banjo, milk shakes)

chewing gum	baseball	rubber balls	mariachi music	piñata
banjo	milk shakes	chia pet	chili	

Which of the following is a word from Mexico?
(Answer: all of them are)

coyote	tomato	cocoa	cafeteria

MIDDLE EAST

Muslim Child: Understanding Islam through Stories and Poems by Rukhsana Khan. Albert Whitman, 2002. (4–5) Eight stories correspond with the major aspects of Islam: belief, prayer, charity, pilgrimage to Mecca, Islamic dress, dietary restrictions, celebrations and the birth of the prophet Muhammad. There are also several poems and pages of sayings of Muhammad and from the Koran. The stories are from a variety of countries (only 20% of Muslims are Arab).

> *"My intention in writing* Muslim Child *was to correct the misconceptions regarding Muslims, and to show the personal side of Islam, by telling stories of everyday Muslim children and their struggles with faith and fitting in." –Rukhsana Khan*

The Persian Cinderella by Shirley Climo. HarperCollins, 1999. (K–4)

NATIVE AMERICAN

Native American Crafts of the Northwest Coast, the Arctic, and the Subarctic by Judith Hoffman Corwin. Scholastic, 2003. (K–5) When students think of Native Americans, they usually picture a member of the Plains tribes. This book will involve them in the culture of the Northwest and Arctic tribes by creating replicas of their artwork.

Cynthia Leitich Author Web Site
www.cynthialeitichsmith.com
Leitich explains her tribe's customs, language and other interesting facets of her life and writing. She has excellent links for students to follow for more information.

PUERTO RICO

Puerto Rico (Globetrotters Club) by JoAnn Milivojevic. Lerner Publishing, 2000. (3–5) Basic introduction to the history, geography, social customs or life, economy and culture of Puerto Rico.

VIETNAM

Vietnam (Fiesta! series). Scholastic Library Publishing, 1997. (4–5) Traditions, foods, games and other customs are explained and illustrated for Grandparents Day (Ong Tao Festival), Ho Chi Minh's Birthday, New Year's Day (Tet Trung Thu) and other holidays. Map of Vietnam and a glossary are included.

Vietnam: Faces and Places by Patrick Merrick. The Child's World, 2000. (3–5) Numerous labeled color photographs illustrate two page spreads on a variety of topics including the people, work, food, pastimes and holidays, as well as many others. Each spread contains a map marked with the places from which the items or people on the page come.

Bibliography

Books:

A

Ada, Alma Flor. *My Name is Maria Isabel.* Simon & Schuster, 1995.

Ajmera, Maya and John D. Ivanho. *Back to School.* Charlesbridge Publishing, 2001.

Ajmera, Maya and John D. Ivanho. *Come Out and Play.* Charlesbridge Publishing, 2001.

Ajmera, Maya and Michael J. Regan. *Let the Games Begin!* Charlesbridge Publishing, 2000.

Ammon, Richard. *An Amish Year.* Atheneum, 2000.

—. *Growing Up Amish.* Atheneum, 1989.

Ancona, George. *Barrio: José's Neighborhood.* Harcourt, 1998.

Andrews-Goebel, Nancy. *The Pot that Juan Built.* Lee & Low Books, 2002.

B

Backstein, Karen. *The Blind Men and the Elephant.* Scholastic, 1992.

Barber, Barbara E. *Saturday at the New You.* Lee & Low Books, 1994.

Bateson-Hill, Margaret. *Chanda and the Mirror of Moonlight.* Zero to Ten Limited, 2001.

Bernier-Grand, Carmen T. *Juan Bobo: Four Folktales from Puerto Rico* (An I Can Read Book). HarperCollins, 1995.

—. *Shake It, Morena! And Other Folklore from Puerto Rico.* Millbrook Press, 2002.

Bial, Raymond. *Amish Home.* Houghton Mifflin, 1993.

Bonnici, Peter. *The First Rains.* Lerner Publishing, 1985.

Bradby, Marie. *Momma, Where Are You From?* Scholastic, 2000.

Brett, Jan. *The Mitten: A Ukrainian Folktale.* Putnam, 1989.

Bunting, Eve. *Dreaming of America: An Ellis Island Story.* Troll Communications, 2001.

—. *Moonstick: The Seasons of the Sioux.* HarperCollins, 2000.

C

Chinn, Karen. *Sam and the Lucky Money.* Lee & Low Books, 1995.

Climo, Shirley. *The Korean Cinderella.* HarperCollins, 1993.

—. *The Persian Cinderella.* HarperCollins, 1999.

Cohen, Barbara. *Molly's Pilgrim.* William Morrow & Co., 1998.

Cole, Joanna. *Bony-Legs.* Scholastic, 1985.

Compestine, Ying Chang. *The Story of Chopsticks.* Holiday House, 2001.

—. *The Story of Noodles.* Holiday House, 2002.

Conrad, Pam. *Blue Willow.* Penguin Putnam, 1999.

Corwin, Judith Hoffman. *Asian Crafts.* Franklin Watts, 1992.

—. *Native American Crafts of the Northwest Coast, the Arctic, and the Subarctic.* Scholastic, 2003.

D

Da Costa, Deborah. *Snow in Jerusalem.* Albert Whitman, 2001.

Demi. *The Empty Pot.* Henry Holt & Co., 1996.

—. *Gandhi.* M. K. McElderry Books, 2001.

E

Enderle, Judith Ross and Stephanie Jacob Gordon. *Something's Happening on Calabash Street: A Story with Thirteen Recipes.* Chronicle Books, 2000.

F

Faber, Doris. *The Amish.* Doubleday & Co., 1991.

Freedman, Russell. *Confucius: The Golden Rule.* Scholastic, 2002.

Friedman, Ina. *How My Parents Learned to Eat.* Houghton Mifflin, 1987.

G

Galdone, Paul. *The Monkey and the Crocodile: A Jakata Tale from India.* Houghton Mifflin, 1997.

Garland, Sherry. *The Lotus Seed.* Harcourt, 1997.

Gershator, David and Phillis. *Bread is for Eating.* Henry Holt & Co., 1995.

Gilman, Phoebe. *Something from Nothing.* Scholastic, 1993.

Gollub, Matthew. *Cool Melons—Turn to Frogs! The Life and Poems of Issa.* Lee & Low Books, 1998.

González, Lucía M. *The Bossy Gallito.* Scholastic, 1994.

Good, Merle. *Reuben and the Quilt.* Good Books, 2002.

Grifalconi, Ann. *The Village of Round and Square Houses.* Little, Brown and Company, 1986.

Grimes, Nikki. *It's Raining Laughter.* Dial Books for Young Readers, 1997.

H

Haley, Gail E. *A Story, A Story.* Simon & Schuster, 1976.

Han, Suzanne Crowder. *The Rabbit's Tail: A Story from Korea.* Henry Holt & Co., 1999.

Harvey, Miles. *Look What Came from China.* Scholastic Library Publishing, 1999.

—. *Look What Came From India.* Scholastic Library Publishing, 1999.

—. *Look What Came From Japan.* Scholastic Library Publishing, 1999.

—. *Look What Came From Mexico.* Scholastic Library Publishing, 1998.

Haskins, Jim. *Count Your Way Through Korea.* Lerner Publishing, 1988.

Herold, Maggie Rugg. *A Very Important Day.* William Morrow & Co., 1995.

Hodges, Margaret. *The Boy Who Drew Cats: A Japanese Folktale.* Holiday House, 2002.

Hoffman, Mary. *The Color of Home.* Penguin Putnam, 2002.

Hooks, Bell. *Be Boy Buzz.* Hyperion, 2002.

Hoyt-Goldsmith, Diane. *Celebrating Chinese New Year.* Holiday House, 1998.

I

Ichikawa, Satomi. *Isabela's Ribbons.* Penguin Putnam, 1995.

J

Johnston, Tony. *The Tale of Rabbit and Coyote.* Putnam, 1998.

K

Kerven, Rosalind. *Aladdin: And Other Tales from the Arabian Nights.* Dorling Kindersley, 2000.

Khan, Rukhsana. *Muslim Child: Understanding Islam through Stories and Poems.* Albert Whitman, 2002.

Kimmel, Eric. *Anansi and the Moss-Covered Rock.* Holiday House, 1990.

L

Lamm, C. Drew. *Gauchada.* Random House, 2002.

Levine, Ellen. *I Hate English.* Scholastic, 1995.

Levinson, Riki. *Watch the Stars Come Out.* Penguin USA, 1994.

Lewin, Ted. *Big Jimmy's Kum Kau Chinese Take Out.* HarperCollins, 2001.

London, Jonathan. *Hurricane!* William Morrow & Co., 1998.

M

Machlin, Mikki. *My Name is Not Gussie.* Houghton Mifflin, 1999.

Mak, Kam. *My Chinatown: One Year in Poems.* HarperCollins, 2001.

McCully, Emily Arnold. *Mirette and Bellini Cross Niagara Falls.* Penguin USA, 2000.

McCurdy, Michael. *An Algonquian Year: The Year According to the Full Moon.* Houghton Mifflin, 2000.

McVitty, Walter. *Ali Baba and the Forty Thieves.* Harry N. Abrams, 1989.

Merrick, Patrick. *Vietnam: Faces and Places.* The Child's World, 2000.

Milivojevic, JoAnn. *Puerto Rico* (Globetrotter's Club). Lerner Publishing, 2000.

Mitchell, Barbara. *Down Buttermilk Lane.* Boyds Mills Press, 2003.

Morris, Ann. *Bread, Bread, Bread.* William Morrow & Co., 1993.

—. *Hats, Hats, Hats.* William Morrow & Co., 1993.

Mosel, Arlene. *The Funny Little Woman.* Penguin Putnam, 1977.

N

Nagda, Ann Whitehead. *Dear Whiskers.* Holiday House, 2000.

—. *Snake Charmer.* Henry Holt & Co., 2002.

Nobisso, Josephine. *In English, Of Course.* Gingerbread House, 2002.

Nye, Naomi Shihab. *Sitti's Secrets*. Simon & Schuster, 1997.

O

O'Brien, Ann Sibley. *The Princess and the Beggar: A Korean Folktale*. Scholastic, 1992.

P

Paulsen, Gary. *The Tortilla Factory*. Harcourt, 1998.

Polacco, Patricia. *Just Plain Fancy*. Random House, 1994.

R

Rappaport, Doreen. *Martin's Big Words: The Life of Dr. Martin Luther King Jr.* Hyperion, 2001.

Recorvits, Helen. *My Name is Yoon*. Farrar, Straus and Giroux, 2003.

Richardson, Adele. *Let's Investigate Nations: India*. The Creative Company, 2000.

Rocklin, Joanne. *Strudel Stories*. Random House, 2000.

Rosa-Casanova, Sylvia. *Mama Provi and the Pot of Rice*. Simon & Schuster, 2001.

Ross, Michael Elshon. *Children of Puerto Rico*. Lerner Publishing, 2001.

Roth, Susan L. *Happy Birthday Mr. Kang*. National Geographic Society, 2000.

S

Say, Allen. *Grandfather's Journey*. Houghton Mifflin, 1993.

Schmidt, Jeremy and Ted Wood. *Two Lands, One Heart: An American Boy's Journey to His Mother's Vietnam*. Walker & Company, 1995.

Scullard, Sue. *The Great Round-the-World Balloon Race*. Dutton Children's Books, 1991.

Shalant, Phyllis. *Look What We've Brought You From Vietnam: Crafts, Games, Recipes, Stories and Other Cultural Activities from New Americans*. Silver Burdett Press, 1988.

Shaw, Janet Beeler. *Kirsten Learns a Lesson: A School Story*. Pleasant Company Publications, 1986.

Shute, Linda. *Momotaro the Peach Boy: A Traditional Japanese Tale*. HarperCollins, 1986.

Simms, Laura. *The Squeaky Door*. Crown, 1991.

Singh, Rina. *Moon Tales: Myths of the Moon from Around the World*. Bloomsbury Children's Books, 2002.

Sneve, Virginia Driving Hawk, ed. *Dancing Teepees: Poems of American Indian Youth*. Holiday House, 1989.

Stalcup, Ann. *American Quilt Making: Stories in Cloth*. Rosen Publishing Group, 2003.

Steptoe, John. *Creativity*. Houghton Mifflin, 2003.

Surat, Michele Maria. *Angel Child, Dragon Child*. Scholastic, 1990.

T

Taylor, Harriet Peck. *When Bear Stole the Chinook: A Siksika Tale*. Farrar, Straus and Giroux, 1997.

Thomas, Jane Resh. *Lights on the River*. Hyperion, 1996.

V

Vietnam (Fiesta!). Scholastic Library Publishing, 1997.

Vuong, Lynette Dyer. *Sky Legends of Vietnam*. HarperCollins, 1993.

W

Waters, Kate. *Lion Dancer: Ernie Wan's Chinese New Year*. Scholastic, 1990.

Wells, Rosemary. *Yoko*. Hyperion, 1998.

Williams, Karen Lynn. *Galimoto*. William Morrow & Co., 1990.

Winter, Jeanette. *Diego: In English and Spanish*. Bantam Doubleday Dell, 1994.

Wong, Janet S. *Apple Pie 4th of July*. Harcourt, 2002.

—. *The Trip Back Home*. Harcourt, 2000.

Y

Young, Ed. *Cat and Rat: The Legend of the Chinese Zodiac*. Henry Holt & Co., 1998.

Z

Zak, Monica. *Save My Rainforest*. Volcano Press, 1996.

Professional Resources:

Allen, Judy, Earldene McNeill, Velma Schmidt. *Cultural Awareness for Children*. Addison-Wesley, 1992.

Champlin, Connie. *Storytelling with Puppets* (second edition). American Library Association, 1997.

Miller, Pat. *Reaching Every Reader: Promotional Strategies for the Elementary School Library Media Specialist.* Linworth, 2001.

Minkel, Walter. *How to Do "The Three Bears" with Two Hands: Performing with Puppets.* American Library Association, 2000.

Orlando, Louise. *The Multicultural Game Book: More than 70 Traditional Games from 30 Countries.* Scholastic, 1995.

Sierra, Judy and Robert Kaminski. *Multicultural Folktales: Stories to Tell Young Children.* Greenwood, 1991.

Stan, Susan, ed. *The World Through Children's Books.* Rowman & Littlefield Publishers, 2002.

Thomas, Rebecca L. *Connecting Cultures: A Guide to Multicultural Literature for Children.* R. R. Bowker, 1996.

Software:

Strategy Challenges: Around the World, Collection I. Edmark, 1995.

Web sites:

Aaron Shepard's Reader's Theater.
Aaron Shepard, 2003.
www.aaronshep.com/rt/index.html

Africa Brainteaser Quiz.
National Geographic Society, 1996–2003.
www.nationalgeographic.com/ngkids/games/
brainteaser/brain.html

Amish Photo Gallery.
Bill Coleman, State College, PA, 2003.
www.amishphoto.com/galleryindex.htm

The Amish and the Plain People.
Pennsylvania Dutch Country Welcome Center, 2003.
www.800padutch.com/amish.shtml

Biography of Mahatma Gandhi.
Biography.com, A&E Television Network, 2003.
search.biography.com/print_record.pl?id=5148

Character Education by the Book.
Scholastic, 2003.
teacher.scholastic.com/professional/todayschild/
charactered.htm

Character Education Resources for Students.
CAEC, Boston University, 2002.
www.bu.edu/education/caec/files/forstudents.htm

Chinese New Year.
University of Victoria (Canada).
www.educ.uvic.ca/faculty/mroth/438/CHINA/
chinese_new_year.html

Connect with Kids and Parents of Different Cultures.
Scholastic, 2003.
teacher.scholastic.com/professional/teachdive/
connectcultures.htm

Countries.
Yahooligans, 2003.
www.yahooligans.com/Around_the_World/Countries

Crayola Card Creator.
Binney & Smith, 2002.
www.crayola.com/cardcreator/index.cfm?mt=
cardcreator

Crayola Creativity Central: Make New Friends.
Binney & Smith, 2002.
www.crayola.com/educators/lessons/display.cfm?id=4
98

Cynthia Leitich Author Web Site.
Cynthia Leitich Smith, 1998–2003.
www.cynthialeitichsmith.com

Dan's Wild Weather Page.
Dan Satterfield, 1997.
www.wildwildweather.com

Deep in the Bush Where People Rarely Ever Go.
Phillip Martin, 1999.
www.phillipmartin.info/liberia/

Discovering China.
Stone Scholastic Academy, 2000.
zone.cps.k12.il.us/Showcase/Student_Projects/China/
china.html

Dr. Martin Luther King Interactive Scavenger Hunt.
Teresa Strong, 1999–2002.
users.rcn.com/tstrong.massed/Martin.htm

Etch-A-Sketch.
Ohio Art Company, 1998.
www.etch-a-sketch.com/html/onlineetch.htm

Folktales on the Web: Internet Field Trip.
Scholastic, 1996–2003.
teacher.scholastic.com/fieldtrp/childlit/folk.htm

Fruit Game.
20/20 Technologies, 1999.
www.2020tech.com/fruit

How to Choose the Best Multicultural Books.
Instructor Magazine, Scholastic, 1996–2003.
teacher.scholastic.com/lessonrepro/lessonplans/
instructor/multicultural.htm

Kids Web Japan.
Japan Information Network, 2003.
jin.jcic.or.jp/kidsweb/index.html

Lower Eastside Tenement Museum.
Kravis Multimedia Education Center, 2000.
www.wnet.org/tenement

Mancala.
Imagiware, Inc., 1999.
imagiware.com/mancala

Multicultural Calendar.
KidLink Society, 2003.
www.kidlink.org/KIDPROJ/MCC

Native American Lore Index.
Stone E Productions, 1996.
www.ilhawaii.net/~stony/loreindx.html

Oriental Trading Company.
Oriental Trading Company, 2003.
www.oriental.com

Peace Corps Kids World: Explore the World.
Peace Corps.
www.peacecorps.gov/kids/world

Peace Corps Kids World: Foods, Friends and Fun.
Peace Corps.
www.peacecorps.gov/kids/like/

Pita Bread
Scholastic, 1996–2003.
teacher.scholastic.com/lessonrepro/lessonplans/ect/pitabr.htm

Plastic Fork Diaries: Food Field Trips.
Maryland Public Television, 2003.
www.plasticforkdiaries.org/fieldtrip/index.cfm

The Puppetry Home Page.
Sagecraft Productions, 2003.
www.sagecraft.com/puppetry

Research Tools: Martin Luther King Jr. and African American History.
Scholastic, 2003.
teacher.scholastic.com/researchtools/article archives/honormlk/index.htm

U.S. Immigration: 1880–1914.
Scholastic, 2003.
teacher.scholastic.com/researchtools/research starters/immigration/

Who Lives on the Moon?
Multiculturalpedia, 1997–2003.
www.netlaputa.ne.jp/~tokyo3/e/

Xpeditions.
National Geographic.com, 2003.
www.nationalgeographic.com/xpeditions/atlas/index.html